THE
NEW YORKER
BOOK OF
CARTOON PUZZLES
AND GAMES

THE NEW YORKER
BOOK OF
CARTOON PUZZLES
AND GAMES

FOREWORD BY
WILL SHORTZ & ROBERT MANKOFF
PUZZLES BY
PUZZABILITY

Black Dog & Leventhal
Paperbacks
NEW YORK

ISBN 10: 1-57912-553-0
ISBN 13: 9-781579-125530

Library of Congress Cataloging-in-Publication Data on file at the offices of the publisher.

Book and cover design by Puzzability

Front cover drawings (clockwise from upper left) by Roz Chast, Lee Lorenz, Jack Ziegler, Bruce Eric Kaplan, Arnie Levin, Leo Cullum, Gahan Wilson, and James Stevenson

Manufactured in the U.S.A.

Published by
Black Dog & Leventhal Publishers, Inc.
151 West 19th Street
New York, New York 10011

Distributed by
Workman Publishing Company
708 Broadway
New York, New York 10003

b d f g e c a

CONTENTS

FOREWORD
THE "AHA" MOMENT
A CONVERSATION BETWEEN
WILL SHORTZ AND ROBERT MANKOFF

Robert Mankoff, the cartoon editor of *The New Yorker*, and Will Shortz, NPR's puzzlemaster and the crossword editor of the *New York Times*, first met—as they say in Hollywood—"cute." Dedicated table-tennis players, they found themselves one evening in 2002 on opposite sides of a small net, paddles in hand. They are both regularly inundated with the work of professionals, amateurs, and wannabes. Each considers it his duty to keep the quality of the work he presides over as high as it can be. Says Mankoff, "All of this—cartoons and puzzles—may be considered the children's table to somebody else, but we're in charge and we want the place settings to be right."

Mankoff and Shortz have a good bit to say about the intersection of puzzles and cartoons—the similarities and differences between two mediums that tickle, perhaps, two different parts of the brain.

MANKOFF: Bringing together cartoons and puzzles is quite natural, it seems to me. Puzzles and cartoons are both respites from the world. Cartoons represent freedom—they're a relief from the crushing monotony and rigidity of the world. Puzzles are a respite from the chaos.

SHORTZ: When I was in high school and we could order books through the book club, there were two kinds of books I always ordered: all the puzzle books, and all the cartoon books. They just go hand in hand to me.

MANKOFF: Of course, people want to be able to solve a puzzle—but maybe they want to "solve" a cartoon, too. I get complaints from people who say, "I don't get some of the cartoons."

SHORTZ: Is that necessarily bad?

MANKOFF: It's not our intention to talk down to our readers. But sometimes we try to push the cartoons beyond the expected—occasionally you have to figure them out. So sometimes they do have aspects of puzzles.

SHORTZ: When the incongruous parts of a cartoon come together, you want them to come together in a rush—a *snap*. That's what produces a burst of laughter. It's the same thing with puzzles. When the solver *gets* it, you want him to get it quickly.

MANKOFF: A cartoon works almost inversely to the way a puzzle works. You do need a knowledge base for both, but in cartoons we're always double-crossing you. We're setting you up with one script and then switching it. We once ran a cartoon in which a female praying mantis is talking to a male praying mantis—but the male is missing his head. She's saying, "You slept with her, didn't you?" Now, everyone knows that praying mantises can't talk ...

SHORTZ: ... but you ignore that.

MANKOFF: And the male would be dead—she bit his head off.

SHORTZ: But you ignore that, too.

MANKOFF: In order for it to be funny, you have to know about the mating behavior of praying mantises. There is something to figure out. We've actually done studies of people reading cartoons in which we track their eyes and measure their pupil size. You might think that reading and understanding a cartoon happens almost instantly, but actually there's a discernible delay. At the moment the reader understands the cartoon, his pupil size increases very fast—about as fast as it can. That's the "aha" moment.

SHORTZ: I try to put as many "aha's" as I can in a puzzle.

MANKOFF: In getting ideas for cartoons and, I'd think, in getting ideas for puzzles—and to some extent for solving them—there is an unconscious process where, the harder you try, the more you have to look away. When I have to get an idea for a cartoon, I'm frozen. So I have to look away. But even though I may be doing something else, my brain is still working on it. When I'm doing other things, my brain becomes free of conflict, inhibitions, the things that block me. In the pursuit of humor, one thing that blocks us is anxiety.

SHORTZ: Yes—you have to be loose with humor.

MANKOFF: I wouldn't think you need to be funny to solve a puzzle.

SHORTZ: I think it helps. I think wit and a sense of humor are very useful, because so many clues are not dictionary definitions. They require a leap of imagination. In solving the puzzles in this book, I'd start with the humor, with figuring out the joke. If I had trouble with that, I'd focus on the letters. And then I'd work back and forth between the two until I got it.

MANKOFF: It's true, these puzzles tap into both sets of skills. The people who are good at wordplay just need a point of entry and they'll be on their way.

SHORTZ: I like to go into a puzzle not knowing how hard it is. And what I think is hard may not be someone else's idea of hard. It's subjective. There's your knowledge base, your mood. People sometimes say, "I couldn't solve the puzzle before I went to bed at night, and in the morning it fell together instantly."

MANKOFF: I would try to understand the puzzle first. Because sometimes not only can I not figure out the puzzle, I can't even figure out the instructions!

SHORTZ: The number-one rule of puzzle-making is, put yourself in the solver's shoes. Understand what can and can't be solved, and what's interesting. And I think in cartooning you always put yourself in the reader's shoes. It doesn't matter if the puzzle or the cartoon breaks rules or not—as long as you're creating a workable situation for the reader.

MANKOFF: At *The New Yorker* I'm looking for cartoonists who break the rules. If cartoons stayed exactly the same over time, Roz Chast never would have been published.

*   *   *

SHORTZ: A daily *New York Times* crossword puzzle is fifteen by fifteen squares, and often the puzzle will have a set of themed answers that span the width of the grid. So crossword constructors are always looking for phrases of fifteen letters. You'll be in conversation with a constructor and you see his eyes sort of go up to the ceiling—he's only half listening to you. He's counting the number of letters in some phrase you just said.

MANKOFF: There's a similarity with cartoonists. We're always listening for a great phrase or seeing something and trying to remember it. Spouses of cartoonists are always complaining that they're never quite all there.

SHORTZ: Cartoonists and puzzle constructors are also similar in that everything they encounter in life is possible material for their work. They can never completely turn it off. Besides ... what we do is fun! We don't want to turn it off.

MANKOFF: You have to keep doing it or you get out of the habit of all that processing. I know when I go for periods where I don't do cartoons, I can't just tap back into it quickly. I haven't done the woolgathering—the work you're doing when it seems as if you're not doing anything but worrying about the work. But really, you're gestating a lot of things. Most of the time you're cartooning, you're not cartooning. You're sitting there *trying* to cartoon. But the idea that you're not doing anything is wrong.

SHORTZ: Most people who have never been involved with puzzle construction have no idea how it's done. The question that a crossword constructor gets asked the most is, "Which comes first, the grid or the clues?" And the idea that someone could have a list of clues and then try to create a crossword based on those clues is just preposterous! Yet with a cartoon it seems obvious. You come up with a joke and then you draw the illustration.

MANKOFF: But that's not always it. Sometimes you'll draw a chicken on a psychiatrist's couch and then start fooling around with that scenario. There's a lot of accidental stuff. You might start one place and end up somewhere completely different.

*   *   *

SHORTZ: The cartoons in these puzzles are all *New Yorker* cartoons. Somehow the gang at Puzzability found, for instance, a six-by-six word square in which all the words could be found in *New Yorker* cartoons. And to solve the puzzle you have to figure out the cartoons. And on top of that—it's funny. It's not just like solving a normal puzzle; it makes you laugh in the end. You'll probably get a whole bunch of laughs from this book.

MANKOFF: There's always a great moment when you're solving a puzzle and you *get* it. It feels good.

SHORTZ: We call it the Cruciverbal Pleasure Center.

MANKOFF: There you go.

SHORTZ: I just made that up.

MANKOFF: I think that one of the nice things about both writing puzzles and making up cartoons is that it glorifies cleverness. In this country we tend to glorify activities like sports, athletic abilities. It hearkens back to a time when someone in the tribe was revered for being able to leap a chasm—to do a physical thing. But what about those other tribe members, the clever ones? They're the ones who tell the athlete the best place to jump.

SHORTZ: Part of the pleasure of doing puzzles like the ones in this book is that, beyond the satisfaction of completing it yourself, you can also look at the completed puzzle and think, "Man, that is elegant. I haven't just solved something, I've discovered something that's really pretty. And I don't know how the people who put this together did it." It's a nice feeling to have, and for puzzle constructors it's a nice feeling to give.

A NOTE FROM PUZZABILITY

Is this a puzzle book or a New Yorker cartoon book?

Maybe, like the famed collision of the chocolate and peanut butter eaters, it's really something entirely its own. You'll find some familiar puzzle types in these pages—like crosswords and acrostics—but many unfamiliar types as well. You'll find easy puzzles and tricky puzzles; verbal, observation, and matching puzzles; and puzzles that defy categorization, even by us.

But what all the puzzles have in common is the cartoons. All the cartoons in this book—and there are nearly 700 of them—were originally printed in *The New Yorker*. We are undoubtedly the only people reading the magazine's cartoon captions to see how they can be plundered.

So solve the puzzles, and enjoy the cartoons. Seems to us that you can't do one without the other. Which brings us, perhaps, to the answer to the question posed above.

This is a puzzle book until you solve the puzzles—then it's a book of *New Yorker* cartoons with pencil marks all over it.

—Robert Leighton, Mike Shenk, and Amy Goldstein

PUZZLES

These thinkers (1–12) have lost their train of thought. Match them with their original thoughts (A–L). **ANSWER ON PAGE 136**

BURNOUT

ROGET'S BRONTOSAURUS

Irst determine the word missing from each caption (1–9) and write it in the correspondingly numbered set of boxes in the grid. One letter from each word has been provided as a clue. When the words have been filled in, read down the two shaded columns to get the caption to the cartoon that accompanies the grid.

ANSWER ON PAGE 136

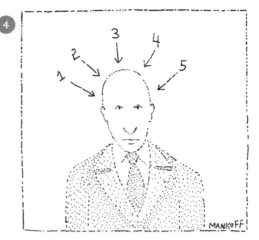

"I bark at everything. Can't go _____ that way."

"Edna! I thought you were in the _____ taking a nap."

"Mildred! Call the _____ —quick! And bring down a bottle of champagne."

The Five Major Warning Signs of _____ .

"Ms. Williams, would you kindly check the _____ hold?"

"You three sit in back. I'll ride _____ ."

"This better be an _____ ."

"What happened to '_____'?"

SOMETIMES A GOOD EXCUSE TO GET OFF THE _____ IS HARD TO FIND.

Each caption here is missing a different five-letter word. When correctly stacked in the grid, the five words will form a word square, with the same words reading down as across, in the same order. Work back and forth to complete the puzzle.

ANSWER ON PAGE 136

"Well, so far I'm managing to stay _____ the fray."

"Too _____ . Use less revenge."

"I think I can get you off with a lighter sentence, but it might screw up your _____ deal."

"Watch where you're shoving that _____ , Mac!"

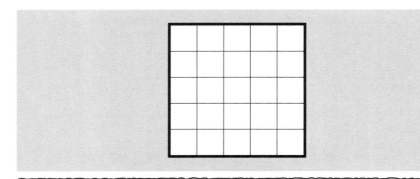

"In our first year of marriage we exposed our _____ , too."

ISOLATION BOOTH

To discover the caption to this George Booth cartoon, look at the seven isolated pieces at right and find them in the large picture. (Some pieces have been rotated.) When you find a piece, write the letter coordinates showing where it came from—putting the column letter in the circle and the row letter in the square. When you've found them all, those letters, in order, will spell out the cartoon's caption.   **ANSWER ON PAGE 136**

5 DESK SET

The little desk signs in these cartoons have been wiped clean. Match each desk (1–13) to its missing sign (A–M). **ANSWER ON PAGE 136**

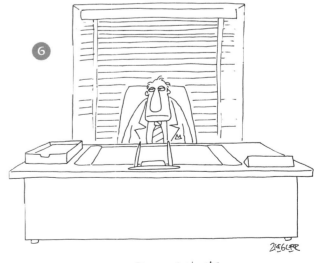

Energy-Efficient Vacation

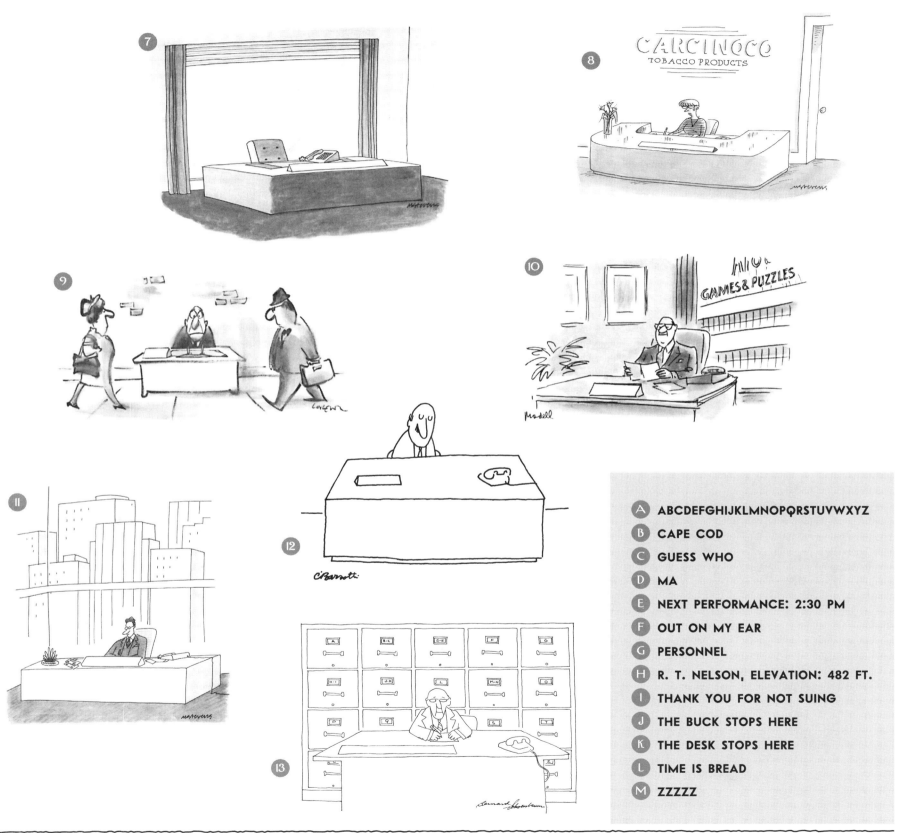

Two four-letter words that are related in some way are missing from the captions of cartoons 1 and 9. Start by entering these two words in the correspondingly numbered spaces in the grid. Then determine the four-letter words missing from the seven other captions here. They can be placed into the intermediate steps so that the word at the top changes into the word at the bottom, with a single letter changing at each step. If you get stuck, try solving from the bottom up. **ANSWER ON PAGE 136**

"Your mother wanted you to have this for good luck. It's her _____."

"Off with my _____!"

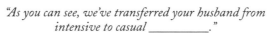

"As you can see, we've transferred your husband from intensive to casual _____."

"_____!"

"We just haven't been flapping them _____ enough."

"I warned you it was lighthearted holiday _____!"

"If it please the Court, I have a get-out-of-jail-free _____."

"We the jury award the plaintiff all the gold in _____ Knox."

"Mitchell— _____ of four."

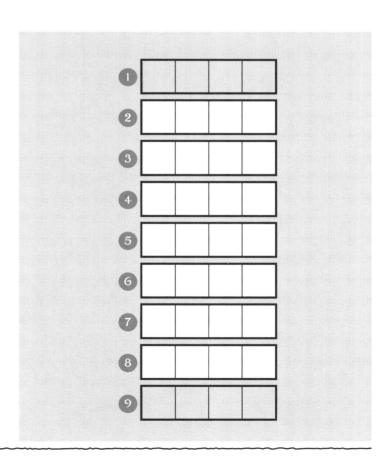

Ten of the answers in this crossword are the missing captions to the cartoons here. Solve the crossword as you normally would, referring to the cartoons where indicated in the clues. **ANSWER ON PAGE 136**

ACROSS

1 Sounds from cartoon readers, perhaps
4 Splinter groups
9 Freshly
13 First name in scat singing
15 Language that gives us "kiwi"
16 Novice
17 [SEE CARTOON]
20 Aimed at the affluent
21 Rents out
22 Ingrid's "Notorious" co-star
23 Groan cause
25 Greetings from guard dogs
28 [SEE CARTOON]
29 Letter opener
33 Potpourri bit
34 Boxers Max and Buddy
36 Wrigley field?
37 [SEE CARTOON]
40 Harp output
41 Is nosy
42 Monopoly purchase
43 Canterbury's county
45 Frivolous gal of song
46 Filmed a second time
47 Go ___ ego trip
49 Easy win
50 Like a capt.'s charts
52 Makeshift bookmarks
55 [SEE CARTOON]
59 "That wasn't supposed to happen!"
60 Perceive
61 Prepare for a match
62 Ready for picking
63 Pool competitions
64 Dirty digs

DOWN

1 This miss
2 Baseball's Moises
3 Trough fill
4 Dirty campaign tactics
5 Before dawn, perhaps
6 Secluded inlet
7 Prefix with angle or athlete
8 Attack command
9 Parthenon setting
10 [SEE CARTOON]
11 Acts human
12 Misery
14 [SEE CARTOON]
18 Seafood item
19 New Haven grad
23 Jury makeup
24 Farming prefix
25 [SEE CARTOON]
26 Writer Zora ___ Hurston
27 When some news airs
28 Tower setting
30 Jim Croce's "___ Name"
31 Like some notebook paper
32 [SEE CARTOON]
34 Tony winner Dennehy
35 Crafty sort
38 ___ Major
39 [SEE CARTOON]
44 [SEE CARTOON]
46 Scoundrels
48 Utmost
49 Hen holder
50 Radar's pop
51 Looking down from
52 Unit of force
53 Workout count
54 Louver piece
55 Stole stuff?
56 Doctrine
57 Ball-bearing item
58 Make tempura

In a captionless cartoon, the drawing does all the heavy lifting, with the "punchline" occasionally taking the form of a single, incongruous detail. In these captionless cartoons, that detail has been removed and placed in the box on the opposite page. Match each cartoon (1–11) with the item (A–K) that belongs in that setting. The numbers show where the missing items originally appeared. **ANSWER ON PAGE 136**

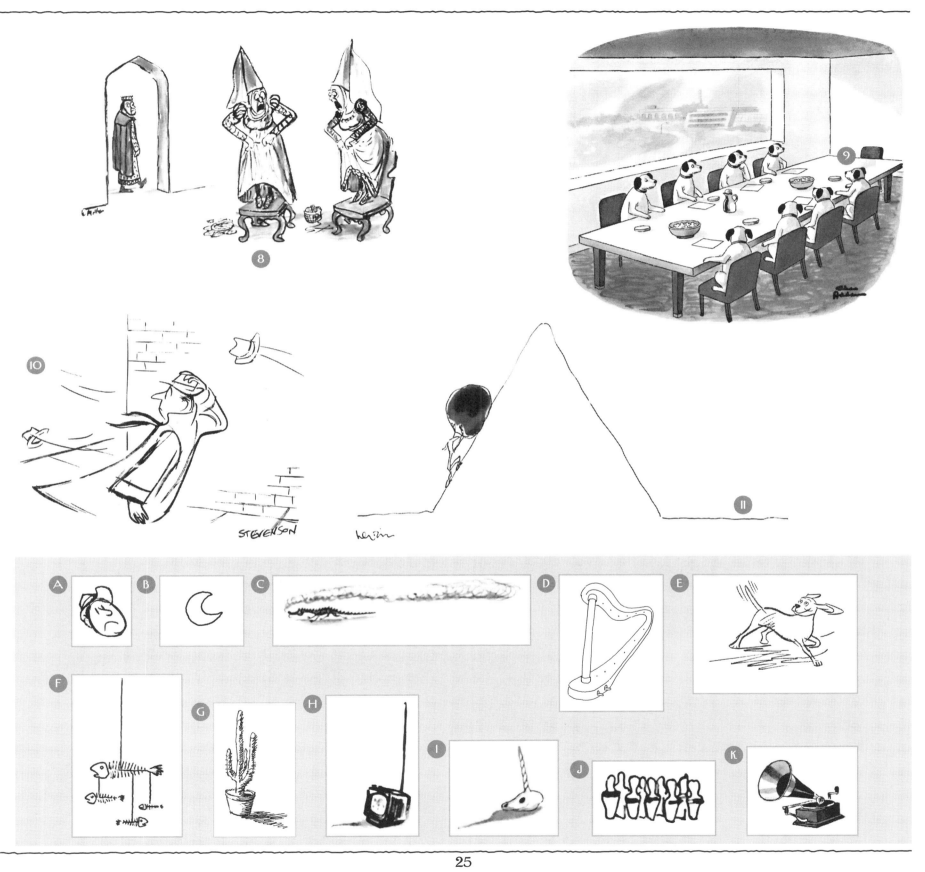

The caption to each bar-related cartoon has been translated into a simple cipher alphabet. For example, everywhere the letter A appeared in the original caption, it might have been replaced with a D, and so on. Letter substitutions remain constant throughout any one caption, but change from one cartoon to the next. Crack the codes to restore each cartoon's caption.

ANSWER ON PAGE 136

1

"TUK JD JC CUQC CUY MYRMIY JZ BUQNFY QITQKD CANZ RAC CR SY JXJRCD? MNYDYZC BRVMQZK, RO BRANDY, YWBYMCYX."

2

"TW XWKVFYKTSW, NKY. E'SS TW USKJ LF WHISKEY LGW NWKYEYU FZ SEZW, TBL YFL JBXEYU XBVG GFBX."

3

"BSIYAU LPSKPJUL VSE DU GMB DZ LIQUEURS, GMB G RAGLL SV OGKUE VSE DZ HB, OJHPJ HL BEHWHMR."

4

"ZLGQ VODKA GQP'Z TDX XSYGPN ZLA BAAW, TSZ FP BAAWAPXQ GZ ZSYPQ GPZF D RFF."

In each caption, two sequential words have been replaced with words that rhyme with the original words. For example, the caption "That's an impressive example of brand loyalty" might appear as "That's an impressive example of canned royalty." The rhyming words can be found together anywhere in the caption, but do not involve incidental words or character names. Restore the captions by replacing the rhymes. **ANSWER ON PAGE 136**

③

"In case they should accept my book, I thought this photo would do nicely for the lust racquet."

②

GRRRRR

"Now, now, Ruffy, if you'll spare me the threats I'll spare you the beagle bargain."

①

"No, I would _not_ care to go out and raid the parrot scratch with you."

④

"Just a heads up, Jack—I've invited the Navy to use my back yard for glomming cactus."

⑤

"Sure, it's an eyesore, but we get wetter slime than anyone else in the neighborhood."

⑥

"This is a daughter crystal—I mean this is a stickup."

⑦

"All righty, then, let's move on to the tech hustles."

⑧

"I found the rolled doormat much more exciting."

One word is missing from the caption to each of these nine cartoons. Fill in the missing words, one letter per blank, and transfer the letters to the correspondingly numbered spaces in the box to fill in a quotation and its speaker. Work back and forth to complete the puzzle.

ANSWER ON PAGE 137

"Once again I'm asking you. How are we going to make our ___ ___ ___ ___ ___ ___ ___ ?"
20 60 46 1 5 51 15

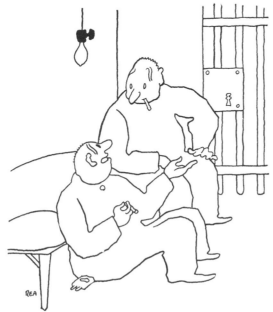

"And then, to make a long story short, I thoughtlessly put a return ___ ___ ___ ___ ___ ___ ___ on the ransom note."
4   17 24 58 34 10 54

"Ah! It's the ___ ___ ___ ___ ___ ___ ___ ___ family!"
26 38 29 2 13 40 49 23

"Don't panic. I'm just a sore ___ ___ ___ ___ ___ ___ ."
41 31 61 48 11 28

COURT

___ ___ ___ ___ ___ ___ ___ ___
50 57 35 22 7   47 12 32

"I can't explain it. I see that guy coming up the walkway
and I go ___ ___ ___ ___ ___ ___ ."
45 25 16 30 19 37

"Oh, how very ___ ___ ___ ___ ___ ___ ."
39 18 53 27 43 56

"Hey, what if marriages had term ___ ___ ___ ___ ___ ___ ?"
33 6   52 9   55 42

"I hear the streets are paved with ___ ___ ___ ___ ___ ___ ___ ."
21 44 3   59 14 8   36

1		2	3	4	5	6	7	8		9	10			
11	12	13	14	15	16		17	18	19	20	21	22	23	
24	25	26	27		28	29		30	31	32		33	34	35	36	37
38	39		40	41	42		43	44	45	46	47	48	49	.
		50	51	52	53	54		55	56	57	58	59	60	61

⑫ MIDDLE MANAGEMENT

Each of the captions on this page (1–7) is missing a five-letter word. Each of those words can be filled into one set of blanks in the captions on the opposite page (A–G) to form the middle of a seven-letter word that completes the caption. The first and last letters of the seven-letter words are provided.

ANSWER ON PAGE 137

① RETIREMENT TRAINING PROGRAM

"Very good, Larry! Just one more step and you'll have the entire _ _ _ _ _ _ blocked!"

②

C'MON, BABY, DO THE LOCO-MOTION...

THE GOOSE THAT LAID THE GOLDEN _ _ _ _ _ _

③

"We'd better stock up on TV snacks in the _ _ _ _ _ _ of war."

④

"I gave you a _ _ _ _ _ _ _ this morning."

⑤

"No caffè _ _ _ _ _ _ ? And you call yourselves a bookstore?"

⑥

"Twisting paper _ _ _ _ _ _ _ . How about you, Ed?"

⑦

"You think you're the only one around here with _ _ _ _ _ _ _ ?"

"When you consider television's awesome power to E _ _ _ _ _ _ _ E, aren't you thankful it doesn't?"

"Poor Al! He had his heart set on being the first American S _ _ _ _ _ _ R to set foot on this soil."

"What I'd like to know, gentlemen, is how the hell we missed the boat on G _ _ _ _ _ _ A rap."

"I tried 911. They're only accepting the S _ _ _ _ _ _ _ H caller."

"It's a whole field of P _ _ _ _ _ _ Y!"

"According to this almanac we should see a total E _ _ _ _ _ _ E next Tuesday."

"That's my cousin's place. I want you to go up there and F _ _ _ _ _ _ N it!"

13 WELL-ORDERED

Put the drawings from this multipanel Claude Smith cartoon back in the proper order.

ANSWER ON PAGE 137

Start by thinking of the four-letter word that's missing from the first caption. Then add a letter and scramble the set to get the five-letter word that's missing from the second caption. Keep adding a letter and scrambling the set at each step, ending with the ten-letter word that's missing from the final caption.

ANSWER ON PAGE 137

"Your fluids are fine, but you've got a slow leak in your left ___ ___ ___ ___ and a hidden explosive device in your right wheel well."

"Hey, ___ ___ ___ ___ ___ Taxpayer, they published your letter!"

"And should you ___ ___ ___ ___ ___ ___ us, Mr. Hodal, you'll find that we're more than just a law firm."

___ ___ ___ ___ ___ ___ ___

"It's your scenario. Mr. Brodkin is ___ ___ ___ ___ ___ ___ ___ ___ the sequence of events."

ETERNAL ___ ___ ___ ___ ___ ___ ___ ___ ___

ZABAR'S
BANANA REPUBLIC — FIRE ISLAND
JEFFERSON MARKET
BLOOMINGDALE'S — EAST HAMPTON
FARMERS' MARKET
MACY'S — JONES BEACH

"For some reason the ___ ___ ___ ___ ___ ___ ___ ___ ___ ___ are not regarding us with the level of awe we were told to expect."

YOU CAN SAY THAT AGAIN

The New Yorker has never knowingly published a cartoon repeating an idea that has previously appeared. But it shouldn't be too surprising that, on occasion, the same caption shows up under completely different cartoons. Match these cartoons (A–N) with the seven captions (1–7), two cartoons per caption.

ANSWER ON PAGE 137

CHRISTIANSON

S. GROSS

1 *"Are we there yet?"*

2 *"But I digress."*

3 *"Ditto."*

4 *"Help!"*

5 *"Surprise!"*

6 *"We'll take it."*

7 *"Will that be all, sir?"*

In the party game of charades, words are often formed by combining small phonetic chunks. In each equation here, the word missing from the first caption plus the word missing from the second caption, when spoken together, will sound like the word missing from the final caption, as in PACE + TREES = PASTRIES. Note that the word's sound, not its spelling, is the key to solving the puzzle.

ANSWER ON PAGE 137

1

"Gimme the _____ and the matching pumps."

"Well, I certainly didn't know this. James Madison only _____ a hundred and twenty-five pounds!"

"In a case of this kind, Mrs. Hall, our first concern is to _____ the patient that he's a stalagmite."

2

"And, like a fool, I said, 'So _____ me.'"

"Well, to make a long story short, she said my lack of _____ was refreshing."

"Perhaps you'd like to visit our _____ shop while you're waiting."

3

"At the risk of being obvious, I'm a talking _____ ."

"Sixty bucks a day this sunshine is costing me, and you have to sit in the _____ !"

"My wife _____ it."

17 TROPHY CASE

Match each setting (1–6) with the trophy (A–F) that belongs on the wall in that setting. The numbers show where the missing trophies originally appeared. **ANSWER ON PAGE 137**

TROPHIES

A   B   C   D   E   F

Each caption here can be completed with a six-letter word, which is to be entered clockwise or counterclockwise around its corresponding number in the grid. The starting point of each word is indicated by a dot, but the direction of each answer is for you to determine.

ANSWER ON PAGE 137

①

"It's publish or _____ , and he hasn't published."

②

"Your family would like to know if you have slaked your _____ ."

③

"Last night's Alpo commercial with Ed McMahon and the Irish _____ was the best thing I've seen on T.V."

④

"Stop—or I'll have a heart _____ !"

⑤

HISTORIC EVENT IN POST-IMPRESSIONISM

_____ WAKES UP TO MEASLES

⑥

"Actually, we're only taking _____ samples."

"I got my _____ for three dollars over the Internet. Are you going to eat that salmon?"

"The _____ story is just that—a story."

"I'll bet you're a _____ . Right?"

"All right, _____ , that's your cue. Come marching in."

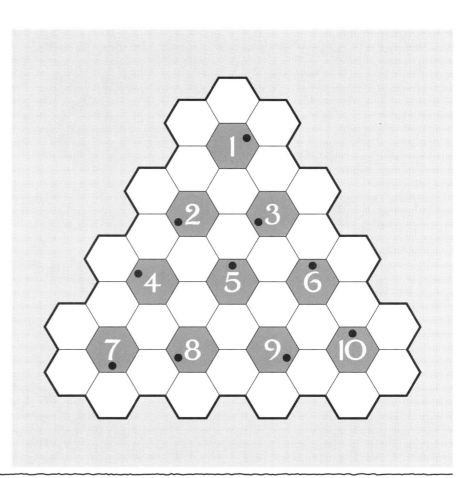

For nearly as long as archeologists have been finding caveman drawings in caves, readers of *The New Yorker* have been finding caveman cartoons in its pages. Match each cartoon (1–15) with its original caption (A–O).

ANSWER ON PAGE 137

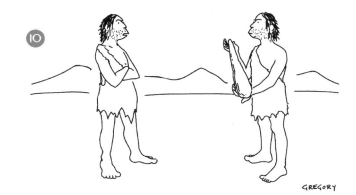

A. "Can't you just be happy for them?"
B. "Cripes, it's the wife!"
C. "Enough storyboarding. Let's shoot something."
D. "Evolution's been good to you, Sid."
E. "Gee, Oolak, I just can't decide. Everything looks so delicious."
F. "I don't know. I'm something of a technophobe."
G. "I think we overordered."
H. "Know what I think? I think you're _way_ ahead of your time."
I. "Let's take it again from 'klonk.'"
J. "Maybe you could make the hunter more likable."
K. "Of course, I haven't got all the bugs out of it yet."
L. "Sometimes spring can't get here soon enough."
M. "We are neither hunters nor gatherers. We are accountants."
N. "Won't you step in and look at my etchings?"
O. "You've got mail."

Drop the letters from each of the vertical columns into the empty boxes below them so that the cartoon's caption will read from left to right, line by line. For example, in caption 1 the letters B, R, I, and G (seen in the grid's first column) will appear in some order in the four blank boxes below them. Black squares indicate the ends of words. **ANSWER ON PAGE 137**

①

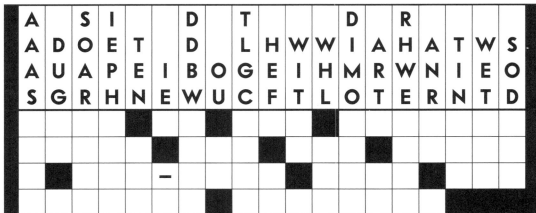

②

S. GROSS

Over the decades, countless *New Yorker* cartoons have touched on TV's pervasive influence—even before that influence became widespread. Each of these cartoons encapsulates a moment in the history of the medium. To solve the puzzle, match each cartoon (1–8) with the decade in which it appeared (1930s–2000s). **ANSWER ON PAGE 137**

1

"'Nantucket Vice.'"

2

3

"If only we could stay home and TiVo the Carlsons."

4

"Come sit beside me, sweetheart. It's our last trip to Marlboro country."

5

"Well, that was better of Brinkley, but now Huntley's flesh tone is off."

6

TV PROGRAMS	TIME
STRIKE IT RICH	MON thru FRI—11:30 A.M.
THE $64,000 QUESTION	TUES—10 P.M.
PENNY TO A MILLION	WED—9:30 P.M.
THE BIG PAYOFF	MON thru FRI—3 P.M.
TWO FOR THE MONEY	SAT—9 P.M.
CHANCE OF A LIFETIME	SUN—9 P.M.

INTERNAL REVENUE SERVICE

7

"They're just late-night talk shows, honey. It's not a real war."

8

"Then everything is settled but the television and doll rights?"

| 1930s | 1940s | 1950s | 1960s | 1970s | 1980s | 1990s | 2000s |

Form a continuous thread of words in the grid by filling in the missing word from each caption, starting in the correspondingly numbered box and proceeding in the direction of the arrow in that box. Whenever you reach an edge, make a right-angle turn, following the direction shown by the arrow at the corner. Each word ends in the box before the next word's number.

ANSWER ON PAGE 137

"Tough day at the _____?"

"Is that an _____ sea horse, or are you just glad to see me?"

"I'm not really a journalist. I just play one on the _____ news."

"You appear to be a _____ young man, but, frankly, we're looking for someone lovable."

"Doris, I'm _____ you."

"And this is our extended _____ room."

"Oh, Kenneth! Your letters never mentioned all these beautiful _____ trees!"

"I've tried Coke and I've tried Pepsi, but I think _____ is best."

"I gotta tell ya, these embezzlement convictions raise a red _____ ."

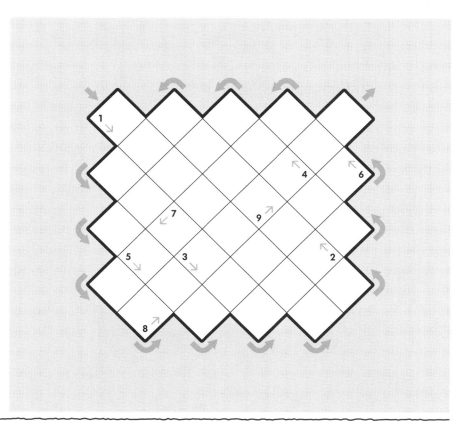

Each caption here is missing a different five-letter word. When correctly stacked in the grid, the five words will form a word square, with the same words reading down as across, in the same order. Work back and forth to complete the puzzle.

ANSWER ON PAGE 137

"If you listen carefully, you can hear the _____ ."

"The couple at Table Three _____ you compliments. However, Tables Six and Fourteen are of a different mind entirely."

"Yes, but take away the rodent droppings and the occasional _____ of glass, and you've still got a damn fine product."

"Come on, honey. We may no longer be 'nouveau,' but at least we're still '_____ .'"

"We _____ the road tonight."

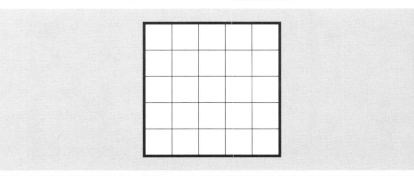

I NEED A CAPTION, STAT!

Leo Cullum's cartoons have visited the doctor's office many times with a surprisingly wide assortment of gags. Match each cartoon (1–8) with its original caption (A–H).

ANSWER ON PAGE 137

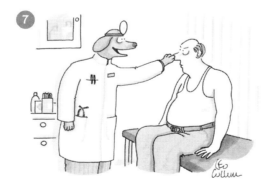

A "Good news. The test results show it's a metaphor."

B "It could be one of those things that crawl into your ear and lay eggs, and the eggs hatch and burrow into your—nope. It looks fine."

C "It is thornlike in appearance, but I need to order a battery of tests."

D "Many women are more at ease with a female doctor. That's why I'm wearing the wig."

E "The ringing in your ears—I think I can help."

F "We could reshape your nose with conventional surgery, but I'm going to suggest something radical."

G "Well, your nose feels cold."

H "You need a transplant, but there are very few good parts for middle-aged women."

First determine the word missing from each caption (1–8) and write it in the correspondingly numbered set of boxes in the grid. One letter from each word has been provided as a clue. When the words have been filled in, read down the two shaded columns to get the caption to the cartoon that accompanies the grid.

ANSWER ON PAGE 137

COFFEE AND A KICK IN THE PANTS
(FORMERLY TEA AND ①)

"You got a letter from MTV. They've been looking at the demographics, and they'd like you to come in for an _____ ."

"Have we got one that says 'Happy _____ Day'?"

"The proof was in the pudding, but the pudding was ruled _____ as evidence."

"Can't we just get some load-bearing _____?"

"The creative director threw me off the account and cut off my _____."

"Please point out when we're passing a _____ so that I can start whistling."

"Surely you can tell _me_ your secret _____."

49

Which saying belongs on each shirt? Match the clean white tees (1–8) with the message (A–H) that's been bleached from each.

ANSWER ON PAGE 138

"It's part of a deal I worked out with the I.R.S."

"Goodness! It never occurred to me that your severance package would include a T-shirt."

A	E
I'M WITH CRAZY	OUT ON MY EAR
B	**F**
LIFE IS A BITCH THEN YOU DIE	I SIDED WITH THE PRESIDENT ON HIS TAX CUTS, BUT ALL I GOT WAS THIS LOUSY T-SHIRT.
C	**G**
SURVIVED THE HOLIDAYS	PROPERTY OF THE U.S. GOVERNMENT
D	**H**
Hard Rock CAFE	SUSSIƆ𝖱AN

In each caption, a letter has been added to each of two words to form new words. The changed words can be found anywhere in the caption but do not involve incidental words. Restore the captions by removing the added letters.

ANSWER ON PAGE 138

"Isn't it wonderful that the prince of chimps hasn't gone up at all?"

"Sorry, but all my power's been turned black to the statues."

"They say there's nothing finger for stimulating the robots."

"He has my noise and his father's ranger."

"A funny thing happened on my wavy into the garbage."

"I understand they melt at a pheasant uprising."

"If I were a czar, you could find the swords."

"Ah, not too bad. Nothing here that monkey can't curse."

Eleven of the answers in this crossword are the missing captions to the cartoons here. (The first cartoon's caption is divided into three entries in the grid.) Solve the crossword as you normally would, referring to the cartoons where indicated in the clues.

ANSWER ON PAGE 138

ACROSS

1 [SEE CARTOON]
5 SAT portion
9 Note after fa
12 Important times
13 Chunnel terminus
15 [SEE CARTOON]
16 [SEE CARTOON]
19 Basic procedures, informally
20 A bunch
21 Stand-in
24 Wimbledon unit
25 Legal rep.
26 Priestly musketeer
28 Bath suds?
29 Cairo Opera House premiere of 1871
33 Like old jeans
34 Future flour
36 Lowest honor card in bridge

37 [SEE CARTOON]
40 Brazil's capital until 1960
41 "Oh, I ___ cry" (Peter Pan declaration)
42 Davis of "Do the Right Thing"
43 He warns, "Beware, my lord, of jealousy"
45 Words before dime or diet
46 English author Edward ___-Lytton
47 Bear in the sky
49 Collar
50 Scrollwork shape
51 "Paradise Lost" character
53 Job site?
55 [SEE CARTOON]
60 [SEE CARTOON]
61 Sings the praises of
62 Saturn, for one
63 Chamonix nix
64 Cafeteria carrier
65 [SEE CARTOON]

DOWN

1 Dawn drops
2 It may be refined
3 ___-di-dah
4 Nicholas II, for one
5 "Le Déjeuner sur l'Herbe" painter
6 "What a shame!"
7 Paver's goo
8 [SEE CARTOON]
9 Flight component
10 Dominates, in sports lingo
11 Auction offering
13 Targets for bulls
14 Plum pudding ingredient
17 Square-dance moves
18 Early Yucatán native
21 Veldt trip
22 Muse of astronomy
23 [SEE CARTOON]
25 Hollywood's elite

27 Most senators
28 Rock concert venue
30 [SEE CARTOON]
31 Turns down
32 Incenses
34 Kofi Annan's homeland
35 Hot water
38 [SEE CARTOON]
39 Fashion monogram
44 Work ___ deal
46 Toyland visitors
48 Croupier's tool
49 Keen
51 Neighbor of TriBeCa
52 "___ for All Seasons"
53 Contemporary of Lon and Boris
54 Panache
55 Salon offering
56 Scratch
57 Broker's suggestion
58 Did lunch
59 Ellipsis unit

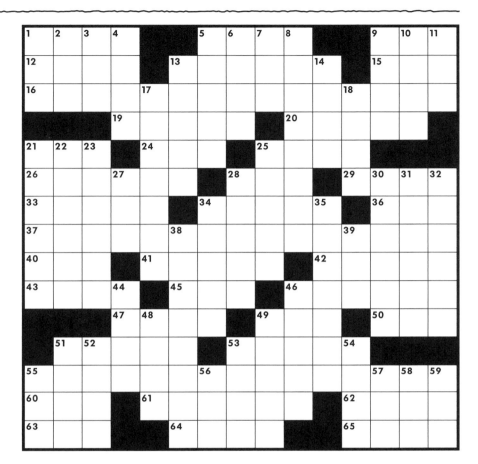

53

Match each cartoon of the Pearly Gates (1–12) with its heaven-sent caption (A–L). **ANSWER ON PAGE 138**

A "A hell of a shot, weren't you?"

B "And I happen to know they won't let you take them with you down there, either."

C "Apparently, it has something to do with el Niño."

D "He's clean."

E "I'd have been here sooner if it hadn't been for early detection."

F "Is there any chance of getting my testicles back?"

G "Let's be reasonable. Just approve my client, and we'll all be spared a lot of nasty litigation."

H "Oh, Freddy! I just knew it would be like this!"

I "Surely you didn't believe what you read in the liberal-controlled press?"

J "The old pearly gates looked nice, but they were hell to maintain."

K "They say the computer is down."

L "You. You. And you."

One word in each of these nine Roz Chast cartoons has been replaced with blanks. Figure out the missing words and fit them into the grid on the opposite page. Then transfer the letters to the correspondingly numbered spaces below the grid to complete the fact. Work back and forth to finish the puzzle.

ANSWER ON PAGE 138

6

CUTE FOR COMFORT

_ _ _ _ _

7 TRICK OR _ _ _ _ _ _

8 BACK WHEN _ _ _ _ _ _ _ WAS KING

Après moi le café!

9 ALL LAWYERED UP AND _ _ _ _ PLACE TO GO

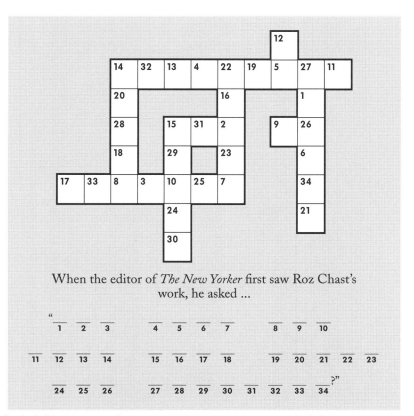

When the editor of _The New Yorker_ first saw Roz Chast's work, he asked ...

"_ _ _ _ _ _ _ _ _ _
1 2 3   4 5 6 7   8 9 10

_ _ _ _ _ _ _ _ _ _ _ _ _
11 12 13 14   15 16 17 18   19 20 21 22 23

_ _ _   _ _ _ _ _ _ _ _ ?"
24 25 26   27 28 29 30 31 32 33 34

57

Match each clown cartoon (1–8) with its original caption (A–H).

ANSWER ON PAGE 138

A "A funny thing happened at work today."

B "And stop trying to cheer me up!"

C "Brightening the lives of passersby without a license, Your Honor."

D "I'm afraid you'll have to be a little more specific, Ma'am."

E "Is everything O.K., sir?"

F "I've asked you all here today to help me develop some really stupid ideas."

G "Just even it out."

H "You will run away from the circus and join a dot-com."

Each letter in each of these captions has been replaced with the same digit every time it appears. You will need only the letters that are given below the coded caption for each cartoon. Use the patterns and word lengths to break each numerical code and reconstruct the caption. Each cartoon uses a different code.

ANSWER ON PAGE 138

"12344 536137 13438?"

ACDELMRS

"122 3 455 34 6785 98554."

AEILMORST

"123 4536 57 8299536."

ACEFLORST

"12 34456 755121846."

ADEINSTV

Each caption here can be completed with a six-letter word, which is to be entered clockwise or counterclockwise around its corresponding number in the grid. The starting point of each word is indicated by a dot, but the direction of each answer is for you to determine.

ANSWER ON PAGE 138

1

"Actually, I preferred '_____,' too, but then the marketing guys got hold of it."

4

"I'd like to _____ a check."

2

"Excuse me, Ma'am, could you please tell me if Spurt is a toothpaste, a detergent, or a breakfast _____ ?"

5

"He said his first word today—'_____ !'"

3

"Since we're both so tired, let's just _____ last night's argument."

6

"The question is, Is _____ electricity better than no electricity at all?"

"Your Honor, I ask you—is this the _____ of a
successful adulterer?"

"How do you get your children not to stick to the
_____ of the cauldron?"

"In my plan, the _____ bomb is used only
for emphasis."

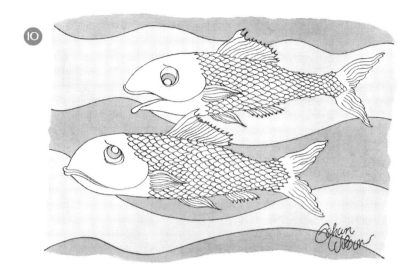

"You've got your _____ on backward."

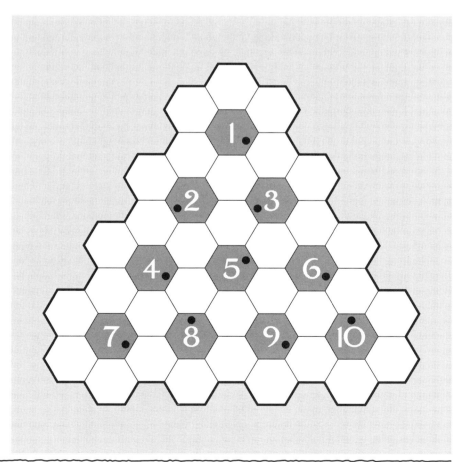

Each of the captions on this page (1–7) is missing one word. In each case, the missing word can be found inserted into a word in one of the captions on the opposite page (A–G), forming a new word. To solve the puzzle, determine each word, both lost and found, that will restore the original captions.

ANSWER ON PAGE 138

1

"I've always been the first to admit that I'm no _____ ."

2

"How do you feel about doing _____ ?"

3

"Tell me frankly, General, do you think I ought to begin saving _____ foil?"

4

"I'll stick with the _____ pork chop."

5

"Miss _____ ."

6

"You keep the _____ out your way. I'll keep it out mine."

7

"I consider myself to be a counterproductive _____ of society."

"Of all the finger-painting classes in all the day-care centimeters in all the world, you had to walk into mine."

"Well, I finally saw that psychiatrist you've been pestering me about, and I give you three guesthouses who's at the root of all my trouble."

"Can you describe this chinchilla shop?"

"Camembert Yummies *again*?"

"What's this, Jenkins? Are you abstinent today or something?"

"Willis *loves* children. He's just a little shrubbery, that's all."

"No, I don't want to play changeless. I just want you to reheat the lasagna."

First determine the word missing from each of these nine captions. The nine words go into the grid in order, one letter per space, starting in the upper left square and spiraling inward. Each answer word overlaps the following answer word by at least one letter, so use neighboring answers to help solve the puzzle. (Every letter is used in two words, except at the beginning of the first word and the end of the last.) When all the answers have been filled in, the shaded column, reading down, will reveal the caption to the cartoon in the box above the grid.

ANSWER ON PAGE 138

"O.K., who has to go _____ before we disappear into the Federal Witness Protection Program?"

"Here we still are, eh? So much for the gloom-and-doom _____ who warned against eating all the vegetation."

"Oh? Well, if _____ is passé, then by all means bring us some of whatever's taken over."

"You're in luck. We have an opening for low man on the _____ pole."

"Could you kindly pick up the _____ a bit?"

"Anti-personnel land mines _____ no threat to <u>people</u>, Colonel. Only to personnel."

"Somewhere along the line, our _____ circle took a strange turn."

"The tiny _____ beings, Sire, are called gnats."

"Sweet? I thought you wanted someone with _____ ."

"_____ ?"

Each caption here is missing a different five-letter word. When correctly stacked in the grid, the five words will form a word square, with the same words reading down as across, in the same order. Work back and forth to complete the puzzle.

ANSWER ON PAGE 138

"_____!"

"I think my indictment was just and when all the _____ are known I will be proven guilty."

"Our stock just went up ten points on the rumor that I was replacing you all with burlap _____ stuffed with straw."

"_____!"

"I just said that for _____ effect."

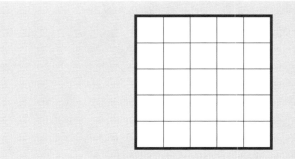

37 MIXED BREED

Put the drawings from this multipanel George Woodman cartoon back in the proper order.
ANSWER ON PAGE 138

M atch each store window (1–10) with the sign (A–J) that belongs in that window. **ANSWER ON PAGE 138**

Two four-letter words that are related in some way are missing from the captions of cartoons 1 and 10. Start by entering these two words in the correspondingly numbered spaces in the grid. Then determine the four-letter words missing from the eight other captions here. They can be placed into the intermediate steps so that the word at the top changes into the word at the bottom, with a single letter changing at each step. If you get stuck, try solving from the bottom up.

ANSWER ON PAGE 139

"Another decade or so, and it'll be _____ enough for us."

"One final question: Do you now own or have you ever owned a fur _____ ?"

"I really can't emphasize this enough, Peters—you no longer _____ here."

"It's never been about money. It's about the _____ stuff money can buy."

"Now who do I see about the sweetheart in every _____ ?"

"I'm sorry, but you have to be here the minute the doors open if you want _____ ."

"Good news—those lumps were just _____ ."

"Your constant cries to cut the _____ sadden me, Senator."

"Why don't you young people play _____ Office?"

"Would it be possible for you to totally exaggerate how much it will _____ and how long it will take, so we'll be pleasantly surprised at the end?"

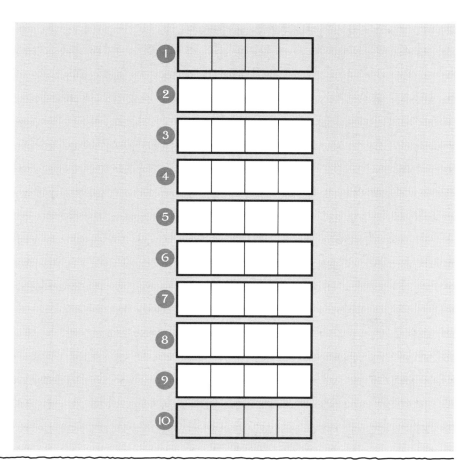

One word is missing from the caption to each of the first five cartoons here. Fill in the missing words, one letter per blank, and transfer the letters to the correspondingly numbered spaces in the box to fill in the caption for the final cartoon. Work back and forth to complete the puzzle.

ANSWER ON PAGE 139

"You've changed, Irma. You used to love ___ ___ ___ ___ ___ marches."
16 6 11 3 20

"Personally, I prefer a ___ ___ ___ ___ ___ bar."
19 1 4 15 10

"Oh, I've stepped on a few ___ ___ ___ ___ in my lifetime."
18 25 9 12

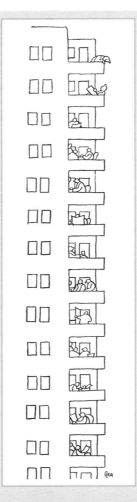

"Five thousand hours, and his vital ___ ___ ___ ___ ___ are still strong."
21 23 8 26 13

"Just clean out the ___ ___ ___ ___ ___ ___ ___ , Tony,
5 14 2 24 17 7 22
and point the chimney."

" ___ ___ ___ , ___   ___ ___ ___ ___ ___ ___ ___ ___
1 2 3   4   5 6 7 8 9 10 11 12

___ ___ ___ ___ ___ ___ . ___ ___ ___ ___   ___ ___   ___ ___ ."
13 14 15 16 17 18   19 20 21 22   23 24   25 26

In each of these captions, the name of a past President has been removed. (Most of the original captions used just the President's last name.) Match each cartoon (1–8) with an answer candidate (A–H) to complete the captions.

ANSWER ON PAGE 139

1

"_____ says he will not raise taxes. That's all I know. That's all you need to know."

2

"Actually, I don't think Dole's administration would have been much different from _____'s— except, of course, for the blow jobs."

3

"President _____ wants to say 'Howdy.'"

4

"What does _____'s being forty-three years old have to do with _your_ being forty-three years old?"

5

"Before _____ came along, you never used to twinkle and say 'Well …'"

6

"I don't so much buy the national-malaise idea per se. My version is: I've got _my_ malaise, _____'s got _his_ malaise, you've got _your_ malaise. We've all of us got our _own_ malaises going."

7

"Your opinions are every bit as salty as his, dear, but _____ was, after all, the President, while you're more or less just a crank."

8

"Well, if Mr. _____ is President, who is Mr. Ziegler?"

- (A) HARRY TRUMAN
- (B) JOHN KENNEDY
- (C) LYNDON JOHNSON
- (D) RICHARD NIXON
- (E) JIMMY CARTER
- (F) RONALD REAGAN
- (G) GEORGE H. W. BUSH
- (H) BILL CLINTON

The captions to each numbered pair of cartoons can be completed with single words that are anagrams of each other. Use both the context and the letters to complete both captions in each pair. **ANSWER ON PAGE 139**

$$\$ = mc^2$$

_____ AT THE BANK

"Well, Al, the sixties was <u>peace</u>. The seventies was <u>sex</u>. The eighties was <u>money</u>. Maybe the _____ will be <u>lumber</u>."

"_____ listen carefully, as the menu has changed."

"Shh! He's _____ ."

"Nice try, Mom, but I'm going to go with a _____ ."

"It just seems to me, Howard, that you're missing the whole point of having a _____ in the city."

"Generally speaking, your novel is quite good, but everyone here feels that the New Orleans _____ scenes lack authenticity."

"Better let _me_ answer that _____ , love— just in case."

"If I told you the secret of making light, flaky _____ , it wouldn't be much of a secret anymore, now would it?"

"You don't look anything like your _____ ."

"A word to the wise, Bodner. In this morning's meeting, you were referred to as 'a certain party who shall remain _____ .'"

"—or you could use it to shoo _____ like me away from the door."

Charles Barsotti's graceful lines and pithily worded captions began making regular appearances in *The New Yorker* in 1968. Since then, his menagerie of kings, lions, and, occasionally, pasta has become closely associated with the magazine. Seven of the answers in this crossword are the missing captions to the Barsotti cartoons here. Solve the crossword as you normally would, referring to the cartoons where indicated in the clues.

ANSWER ON PAGE 139

ACROSS

1 [SEE CARTOON]
6 Lady's man
10 Breath mints buy
13 Touches on
14 Record holder?
16 Capitalize on
17 [SEE CARTOON]
20 Its business is pressing
21 Assigned stars to
22 Cry of insight
25 "That's really something!"
26 Fellow with a handle
28 Some vacation homes
30 [SEE CARTOON]
34 Cover for Cato
35 Get better
36 Director Howard
37 [SEE CARTOON]

42 Simple card game
43 Physicist's study
44 "The ___ Love" (R.E.M. hit)
45 [SEE CARTOON]
47 Looks forward to
49 They sometimes clash
50 Low digit
51 Cabin bed
52 Brushy wasteland
55 Right upstairs
56 [SEE CARTOON]
63 Buffalo-to-Baltimore dir.
64 Portuguese territory until 1999
65 Writer Calvino
66 Scandal subject
67 Score unit
68 [SEE CARTOON]

DOWN

1 Existed
2 "The Sopranos" carrier
3 "That's tasty!"
4 A-train org.
5 Language group including Inuit
6 Zest source
7 Cart pullers
8 Its ads feature Nipper
9 King of boxing
10 Clump of grass
11 Shrink's reply
12 Bully's target, often
15 1964 Beatles song
18 Chapters of history
19 Jamie of "M*A*S*H"
22 When Juliet asks, "Wherefore art thou Romeo?"
23 Noisy controversy
24 Ticks off
26 Threw a line, perhaps
27 "Dracula" author Stoker
29 Work period

30 Brother of Moe and Curly
31 Like O. Henry endings
32 Site of 1976 apartheid riots
33 Sign up
38 "The Razor's Edge" writer
39 Bus driver on "The Simpsons"
40 *"Parlez-___ français?"*
41 Flapper wrapper
46 Eighth Hebrew letter
47 First-rate
48 Plant pest
50 Resort east of Squaw Valley
52 Disapproving sound
53 Different
54 Baseball's Rodriguez
55 ASAP in the OR
57 Moving vehicle
58 Earth-friendly prefix
59 Pilot's guess: Abbr.
60 Gangster's gun
61 Heady brew
62 Negative connector

77

Each of the cartoons here appeared between 1957 and 1971, as computers began to do more and more of our thinking—and before they became small enough to fit into our shirt pockets. Match each cartoon (1–8) with its original caption (A–H).

ANSWER ON PAGE 139

A "Damn you, Winkle, did you have to go and ask it which came first—the chicken or the egg?"

B "In case of power failure. We like to think ahead."

C "It says *I'm* the fairest one of all! So there!"

D "Just as I thought! It's been lying to us!"

E "Just listen to all that whirring and buzzing and clicking, and not a single demand for a raise!"

F "Knock it off, you two! Time to get back to work."

G "Now, here's an earlier model I can give you a real buy on."

H "Please, Charles, not here!"

The caption to each royal cartoon has been translated into a simple cipher alphabet. For example, everywhere the letter A appeared in the original caption, it might have been replaced with a D, and so on. Letter substitutions remain constant throughout any one caption, but change from one cartoon to the next. Crack the codes to restore each cartoon's caption.

ANSWER ON PAGE 139

"RIXKMYH FH MR M

GIB'U VPLCH PLBGV.

HYHXEUPMBK M UISZP

NLUHNE USXBV UI KING."

"WN ZU, WMU OMNQU

WMYSP MIE LUUS IS NLRUGW

QUEENS YS WMU VYDDUHUSGU

LUWOUUS MFZNH ISV

EIWYHU."

"P XEAL XYT FEEW P REGAL

CBTOTB XYSX QYT GQT

QEUT WPDL EO SBXPOPFPSA

HASFWHPBL QGHQXPXGXT."

"GTHH, UY KMD GME'N

OAVUJONT, NST HTORN

KMD JOE VM UR COURT ZK

OHHMGOEJT."

First determine the word missing from each caption (1–9) and write it in the correspondingly numbered set of boxes in the grid. One letter from each word has been provided as a clue. When the words have been filled in, read down the two shaded columns to get the caption to the cartoon that accompanies the grid.　ANSWER ON PAGE 139

"How are you at digging _____?"

"I can lick any man within _____!"

"I knew about the wings, but the _____ feet are a surprise."

"I'm ruined! They've plugged my _____!"

"How can I work with you constantly looking over my _____?"

"I've got this _____-of-the-universe gig."

"Let me through! I'm a _____ ."

"Then it's agreed. Judgment Day, whenever it comes, will fall on a Thursday, so that they'll get the long _____ ."

"Why don't you go back to your house for _____ and coffee?"

One word is missing from the caption to each of these eleven cartoons. Fill in the missing words, one letter per blank, and transfer the letters to the correspondingly numbered spaces in the box to fill in a quotation and its speaker. Work back and forth to complete the puzzle.

ANSWER ON PAGE 139

"I'll give it to you straight, Babcock. You lack the

killer $\overline{50}\ \overline{38}\ \overline{16}\ \overline{29}\ \overline{1}\ \overline{22}\ \overline{66}\ \overline{79}$."

"Keep it under your hat, but when this crowd thins out, I have some

$\overline{9}\ \overline{37}\ \overline{18}\ \overline{68}\ \overline{42}\ \overline{26}\ \overline{53}\ \overline{73}\ \overline{74}\ \overline{48}\ \overline{61}\ \overline{30}$."

"When my time comes, I hope I can go with that same air of

jaunty $\overline{10}\ \overline{54}\ \overline{67}\ \overline{47}\ \overline{2}\ \overline{17}\ \overline{60}$."

"Más $\overline{12}\ \overline{82}\ \overline{28}\ \overline{19}$ for the gringos?"

"That's pork—the meat of the pig. It makes an excellent

substitute for $\overline{58}\ \overline{4}\ \overline{45}\ \overline{34}$."

"Fill'er up with $\overline{15}\ \overline{52}\ \overline{24}\ \overline{55}\ \overline{70}\ \overline{63}\ \overline{35}\ \overline{6}\ \overline{49}\ \overline{40}\ \overline{27}\ \overline{80}$."

"Sorry, Akhet, but we've decided to stick with

___ ___ ___ ___ ___ ___ ___ ___ ."
64 44 11 46 77 21 3 57

"Gentlemen, it's time we gave some serious thought to the effects

of global ___ ___ ___ ___ ___ ___ ___ ."
71 31 7 43 56 13 39

Henry ___ ___ ___ ___ discloses his dream life to a psychoanalyst.
      36 75 65 81

"It's the people ___ ___ ___ ___ ___ ___ ___ ___ ___ ___ again."
                 14 33 20 59 69 51 76 25 5 78

"I'm right on the fringe of a ___ ___ ___ ___ ___ ___ , R.B. I'm just
                              32 72 23 41 62 8
waiting for it to jell."

1		2	3	4	5	6		7	8	9	10	11	12	13	14	15	16
17	18	19	20	21	22	23	24	25	26		27	28	29	30
31	32	33	34	35		36	37	38		39	40	41	42		43	44
45	46	47	48	49	50	51	52		53	54	55	56	57	58
59	60	61		62	63		64	65	66	67	68	69	70
	71	72	73	74	75	76	77		78	79	80	81	82

Match the sleepers (1–10) with the sheepish imagery (A–J) they used to drift off to sleep.

ANSWER ON PAGE 139

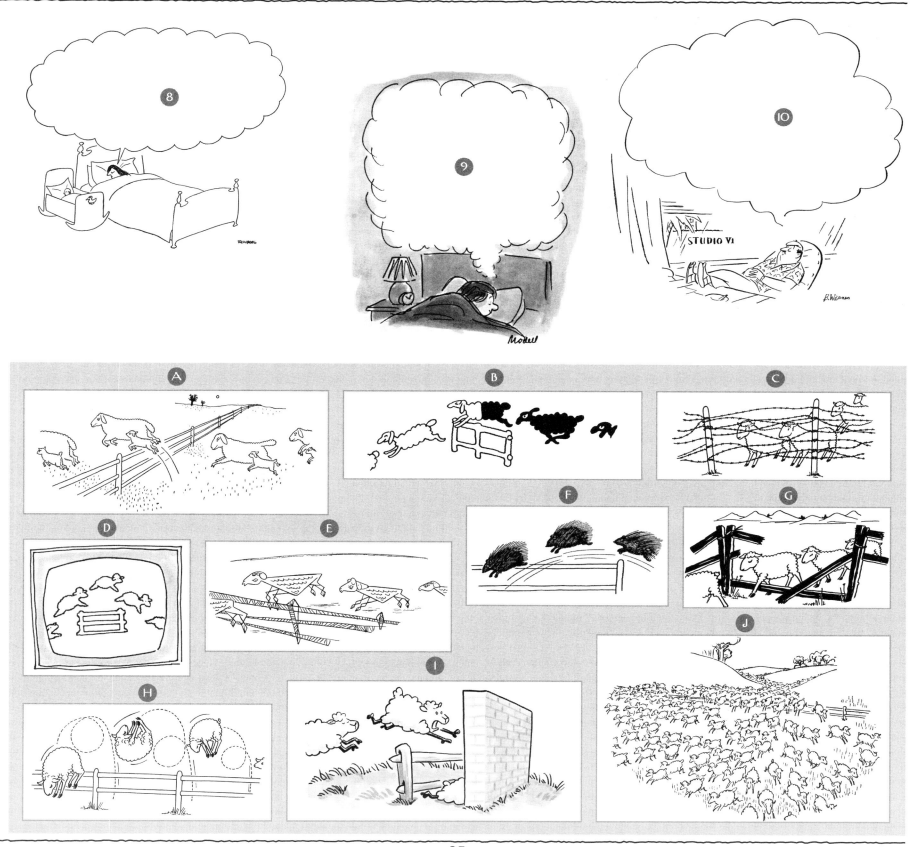

Start by thinking of the three-letter word that's missing from the first caption. Then add a letter and scramble the set to get the four-letter word that's missing from the second caption. Keep adding a letter and scrambling the set at each step, ending with the ten-letter word that's missing from the final caption.

ANSWER ON PAGE 139

(1)

"Oh sorry, those are the __ __ __ Commandments. Hang on, I'll get you a menu."

(2)

"Oh, sure, I remember him. He was quiet, mostly kept to himself, paid the __ __ __ __ on time. You know, we were only married for sixteen years."

(3)

"Decaf's out of __ __ __ __ __ __."

(4)

"I want two days and one dazzling night on the __ __ __ __ __ __ Express!"

(5)

"For God's sake, Edwards. Put the laser __ __ __ __ __ __ __ __ away."

(6)

"You're not getting enough __ __ __ __ __ __ __ __ __."

(7)

"Hey, I'm the building __ __ __ __ __ __ __ __ __ __. This building O.K.?"

(8)

"This has been quite a season for Zobrowsky—a hundred and twenty-nine __ __ __ __ __ __ __ __ __ __, sixteen touchdowns, a B-plus in English, a B in philosophy, an A in political science, and a B-minus in French!"

Drop the letters from each of the vertical columns into the empty boxes below them so that the cartoon's caption will read from left to right, line by line. For example, in caption 1 the letters F, I, R, and W (seen in the grid's first column) will appear in some order in the four blank boxes below them. Black squares indicate the ends of words. **ANSWER ON PAGE 140**

1

Letter source columns (caption 1):

F	E			O	N	A			L				F		G	A		C		A
I	E	A	B	O	O	T	E	I	C	C	I	D	I	O	I	A	J	M	E	I	C	A	G	N
R	H	C	O	E	T	R	S	N	T	R	S	A	N	T	M	M	S	E	I	A	N
W	T	W	T	N	S	U	R	U	S	A	Y	F	R	S	R	S	T	U	Z	T	T	S

2

Letter source columns (caption 2):

T	O	E		E	L		T				T		H	N		I	A	D
T	H	T	E	I	R	R	D	O	I	H	S	L	O	C	I	E	I	N	S
Y	E	E	E	L	W	I	G	R	N	O	K	C	T	R	A	R	H	S	T	N	S
Y	H	U	R	D	A	A	N	E	H	F	N	A	I	S	I	O	T	Y	A	A	S	S

Yōu can restore the captions to these cartoons by forming a chain of compound words. When you determine a missing word, use its second half as the first half of the missing word in the caption of the next numbered cartoon. For example, PICKPOCKET might be followed by POCKETBOOK. The chain will form a closed loop, ending where you began, so you can work in both directions to complete the puzzle. **ANSWER ON PAGE 140**

"Never, ever, think _____ the box."

"You realize, of course, that if you take this position you'll be my _____ ?"

"Does Medicare take care of your _____ ?"

"Gruelling as this is, it's not a total-body _____ ."

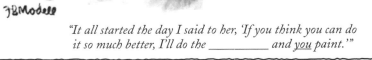

"It all started the day I said to her, 'If you think you can do it so much better, I'll do the _____ and you paint.'"

"He has a good _____ , but you've got to watch him on the scoring."

"I should like to buy a _____ while it is still legal," said Alice very gently.

"At first, I thought it was _____ ."

"What ever became of the days, Béla, when we all used to dance with wild abandon by _____ ?"

"Don't yell at me! I'm no _____ !"

Jack Ziegler is the master of the labelled cartoon, frequently beguiling readers with a seemingly nonsensical drawing that is explained in its boxed "subtitle." Match these Ziegler cartoons (1–16) with their missing labels (A–P).

ANSWER ON PAGE 140

A. BATTLESTAR GALÁPAGOS
B. THE BLACK HOLE OF MESSAGES
C. THE COUP
D. THE CUBICLE OF DR. CALIGARI
E. FACTOMINIUMS
F. HELL ON TRIO ISLAND
G. INSOMNIA
H. JIMMY, SIXTH-GENERATION PAIN IN THE ASS

I. THE JUILLIARD AIR QUARTET
J. THE LOST CONTACT LENSES OF THE GODS
K. THE OLD ROCKETTES' HOME
L. SIMPLER TIMES
M. A SURPRISE GUEST
N. TOUGH COMMUTE
O. TROUBLE AHEAD
P. X-TREME CONVERSATION

9.

10.

11.

12.

13.

14.

15.

16.

Each caption here is missing a different six-letter word. When correctly stacked in the grid, the six words will form a word square, with the same words reading down as across, in the same order. Work back and forth to complete the puzzle.

ANSWER ON PAGE 140

"Sure I told you not to worry your _____ little head about money, but that was ten years ago."

"And to whom do you wish to leave the bulk of your _____ , sir?"

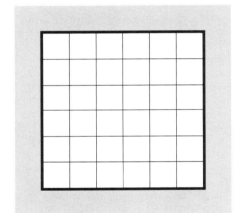

"Eddie is under house _____ ."

"_____ injection's my favorite, because they don't make you shave your head."

"Why have we come? Because only Earth offers the rock-bottom prices and wide selection of men's, women's, and children's clothing in the _____ and sizes we're looking for."

"I don't want to seem nosy, folks, but those aren't sugar _____ ."

These two George Price drawings may seem identical, but there are actually nine differences between them. When you find a difference, draw a straight line connecting the item in the top picture to its changed counterpart in the bottom picture. (You may want to use a ruler.) Each line you draw will cross through a circle with a letter. When you're done, the leftover letters, in order, will spell the cartoon's caption. **ANSWER ON PAGE 140**

What were they thinking? Match the thinkers (1–9) with the subjects of their thoughts (A–I).

ANSWER ON PAGE 140

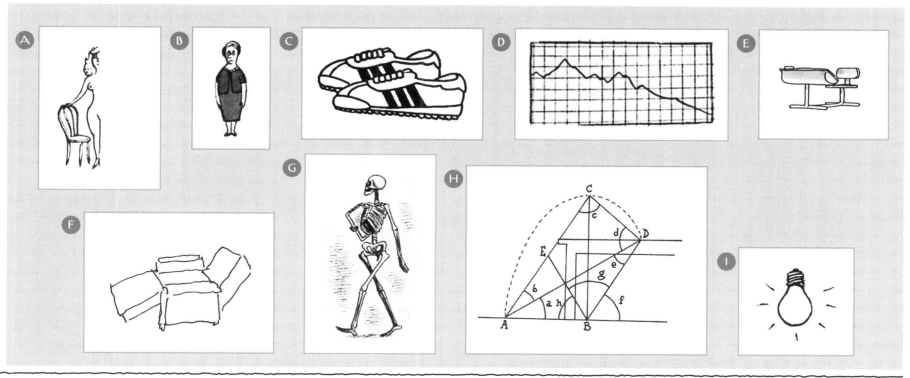

Two four-letter words that are related in some way are missing from the captions of cartoons 1 and 10. Start by entering these two words in the correspondingly numbered spaces in the grid. Then determine the four-letter words missing from the eight other captions here. They can be placed into the intermediate steps so that the word at the top changes into the word at the bottom, with a single letter changing at each step. If you get stuck, try solving from the bottom up.

ANSWER ON PAGE 140

"But she'll come down eventually, and she'll come down _____ ."

"He makes it look so damn _____ ."

"That's the first time I've heard 'My Way' played on a _____ ."

"The minute I saw this _____ , Mrs. Mugler, I thought of you."

"Would you like to take your old _____ ?"

"No, no, Agnes! This is mine. _You_ paid the bus _____ ."

"Perhaps Monsieur would _____ for something more expensive?"

"Burglars, con men, and swindlers all over the place, and I have to marry a lousy accessory after the _____ ."

"Gosh, is this part of the all-expense Middle _____ tour?"

"Somehow they don't seem to be selling as _____ as they should."

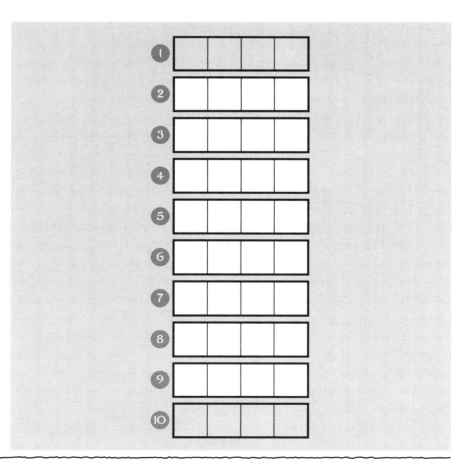

Eleven of the answers in this crossword are the missing captions to the cartoons here, each of which is a single word. Actually, it is a single WORD! because each caption originally ended with an exclamation point. Solve the crossword as you normally would, referring to the cartoons where indicated in the clues.   **ANSWER ON PAGE 140**

ACROSS

1 Maker of Dakotas and Durangos
6 [SEE CARTOON]
10 Pipe material
13 How some sardines are packed
14 Writer Seton
15 Elisabeth of "Leaving Las Vegas"
16 [SEE CARTOON]
18 Bench presser's pride
19 "The Swedish Nightingale"
20 Ballerina's pivot
21 Geological stretches
23 Fox of folktales
25 Boat measured in cubits
26 Fireworks viewer's reaction
27 Natalie of "Closer"
31 Hen holders
34 "See ya!"
36 It's a long story
37 NYPD alert
38 [SEE CARTOON]
41 Barge pusher
42 Punjab prince
44 Tight set
45 Follows the leader
47 Holy
49 PC part
50 Series set in Las Vegas
51 Man with a mission
55 Dress
58 Neither partner
59 Disney collectibles
61 Reagan's first Secretary of State
62 [SEE CARTOON]
65 Impulse carrier
66 Secluded spot
67 Perfect Sleeper maker
68 Storage container
69 [SEE CARTOON]
70 Jon of "Two and a Half Men"

DOWN

1 Havarti additive
2 Studio sign
3 "No man is an island" poet
4 [SEE CARTOON]
5 Angled pipe
6 Big voting bloc
7 Retired
8 Ensign's answer
9 Delmonico's order
10 [SEE CARTOON]
11 [SEE CARTOON]
12 Porgy's love
15 Newspaper section
17 Jazz setting
22 Course goal
24 Political cartoonist Thomas
27 Settles the bill
28 Fireworks viewer's reaction
29 1943 Van Johnson movie "___ Named Joe"
30 Chronic complainers
31 Atkins Diet no-no
32 Milky stone
33 [SEE CARTOON]
34 Not nude
35 Under the weather
39 Big brute
40 Klutz's cry
43 Give as a duty
46 [SEE CARTOON]
48 Baronet's title
49 Mawkish material
51 Photographer Adams
52 Stray's place
53 Guarded
54 Preferred few
55 Giver of Starbuck's orders
56 [SEE CARTOON]
57 Soufflé start
60 Kindergarten award
63 "Telephone Line" band
64 Mil. medal

One word is missing from the caption to each of the first five cartoons here. Fill in the missing words, one letter per blank, and transfer the letters to the correspondingly numbered spaces in the box to fill in the caption for the final cartoon. Work back and forth to complete the puzzle.

ANSWER ON PAGE 140

"It's a little present I gave myself for being so ___ ___ ___ ___ *."*
36 38 12 8

"How about conjuring up something to take the drudgery

out of ___ ___ ___ ___ ___ ___ ___ *?"*
4 37 40 13 28 23 6

___ ___ ___ ___ ___ ___ ___ ___ ___ ___ ___
9 15 22 20 27 34 30 2 18 35 25
JUST WANT TO HAVE FUN · · · ·

"I give him two more minutes. Then I say so

much for ___ ___ ___ ___ ___ ___ ___ ___ ___ ___ ___ *!"*
26 33 3 32 16 1 24 11 19 21 7

"I can see you drew ___ ___ ___ ___ ___ ___ ___
31 17 5 10 14 39 29
from your own bad writing."

"___
1
___ ___ ___ ___ ___ ___ ___ ___ ___ ___
2 3 4 5 6 7 8 9 10 11

___ ___ ___ ___ ___ ___ ___ ___ ___ ___
12 13 14 15 16 17 18 19 20 21

___ ___ ___ ___ ___ ___ ___ ___ ___ ___ ___
22 23 24 25 26 27 28 29 30 31 32

___ ___ ___ ___ ___ ___ ___ ___ ."
33 34 35 36 37 38 39 40

Perhaps few inventions have changed as much over the years as the telephone. Each of these cartoons encapsulates a moment in the history of this ubiquitous device. To solve the puzzle, match each cartoon (1–8) with the decade in which it appeared (1930s–2000s). **ANSWER ON PAGE 140**

1

"We're from the F.B.I. Do you people know you're driving us crazy? You carry on the most inane telephone conversations we've ever been forced to listen to."

2

"I love the convenience, but the roaming charges are killing me."

3

"Once and for all get this straight—I am not to be used for personal calls."

4

BEEP	BEEP	BOOP
BOOP	BEEP	BOOP
BEEP	BOOP	BEEP
BEEP	BOOP	BOOP

P. Steiner

5

6

"I tell you I did try to phone. Could I help it if the booth had seventeen college students in it?"

7

"Can you hang on a sec? I think I just took another picture of my ear."

8

"You're wanted on the phone, Miss McCardy."

1930s	1940s	1950s	1960s	1970s	1980s	1990s	2000s

In a captionless cartoon, the drawing does all the heavy lifting, with the "punchline" occasionally taking the form of a single, incongruous detail. In these captionless cartoons, that detail has been removed and placed in the box on the opposite page. Match each cartoon (1–11) with the item (A–K) that belongs in that setting. The numbers show where the missing items originally appeared.

ANSWER ON PAGE 140

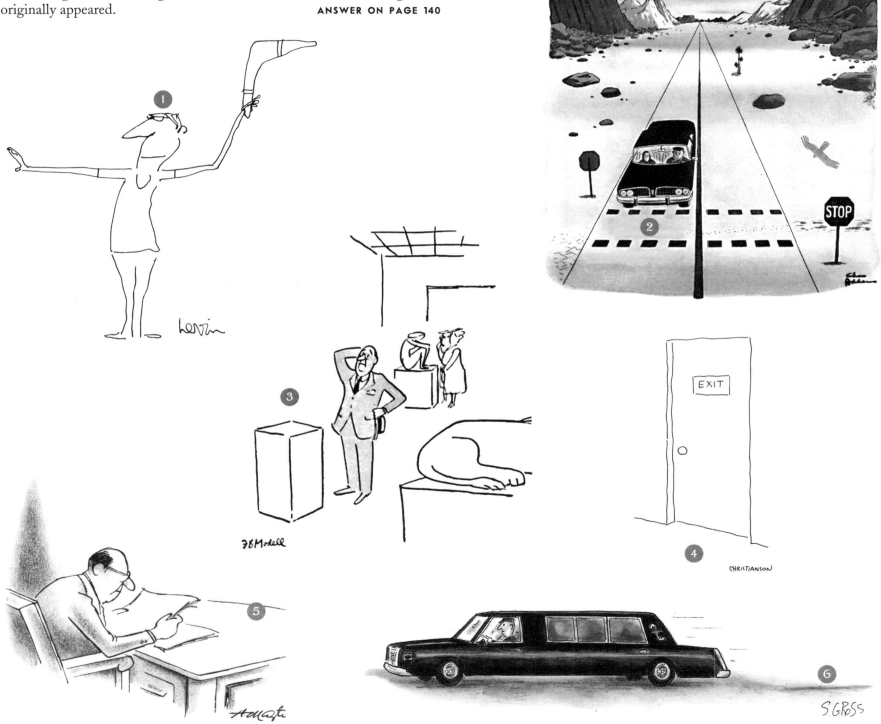

Each letter in each of these captions has been replaced with the same digit every time it appears. You will need only the letters that are given below the coded caption for each cartoon. Use the patterns and word lengths to break each numerical code and reconstruct the caption. Each cartoon uses a different code.

ANSWER ON PAGE 140

"123 342 4251678 92867!"

ABEGHILNT

"123 45567 587 49481!"

AEGILNOPT

"123415 623 7234 6118."

AEKLRSTW

"122345245 16 23 574865."

CEINOSUX

In each caption, two sequential words have been replaced with words that rhyme with the original words. For example, the caption "That's an impressive example of brand loyalty" might appear as "That's an impressive example of canned royalty." The rhyming words can be found together anywhere in the caption, but do not involve incidental words or character names. Restore the captions by replacing the rhymes. **ANSWER ON PAGE 141**

"Dirty phrase. And, by the way, that was a very nice rendition of 'Feelings.'"

"Trickery joke—that's what gives it that hearty Western flavor."

"I'm writing my autobiography, to set the checkered plate."

"Gee, Tommy, I'd be lost without your constant gear thresher."

"Oh, definitely, I feel there's a reason I was given a reckoned trance."

"Melanie, this is my husband, Greg, and Greg's jacket from a devious carriage."

"Every year a mumble leopard! Can't he ever be one of the kings?"

"No, we aren't experiencing low motor burnout. Everybody's here."

Restore these endearingly tasteless Sam Gross cartoons by matching each one (1–14) with its correct caption (A–N).

ANSWER ON PAGE 141

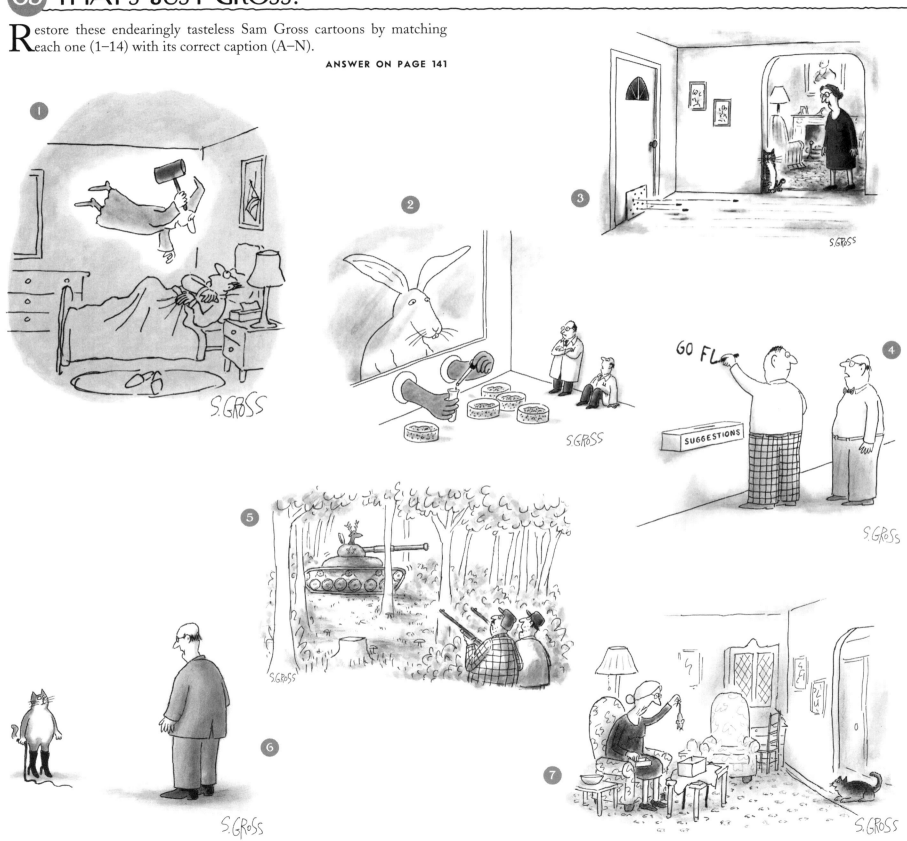

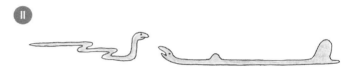

A. "Does the N.R.A. know about this?"

B. "Everything I eat goes straight to my ass."

C. "For God's sake, think! Why is he being so nice to you?"

D. "He had a hat!"

E. "Help! I've fallen and I can't get up!"

F. "I guess we'd be considered a family. We're living together, we love each other, and we haven't eaten the children yet."

G. "J'accuse!"

H. "Look what they did to her! We should be thankful they only had us spayed."

I. "Read the card! Read the card!"

J. "Some genetic engineers we turned out to be!"

K. "Sorry about this, but I just ran out of sand."

L. "The suggestions are supposed to go in the box."

M. "This is not the Puss in Boots I knew and loved as a child."

N. "What kind of mischief are you into now?"

Put the drawings from this multipanel David Langdon cartoon back in the proper order.   **ANSWER ON PAGE 141**

For each of the first five cartoons here, a section of the caption has been replaced with a number. The missing letters will not only complete the caption but will also spell a new word when the spaces are eliminated. For example, the letters missing from "Seems as though I ma ① ittle mistake" would be "de a l," which complete the phrase "Seems as though I maDE A Little mistake" and also spell the word DEAL when the spaces are removed. Each of the five words formed in this manner can then be entered in their correspondingly numbered spots to spell out the caption for the final cartoon. **ANSWER ON PAGE 141**

"I sleep half t ① ear—how much more space do you need?"

"Straighten tha ② oldier! Button that collar! I have spoken."

"How can y ③ ead that garbage?"

"Wow! Dig the umbrel ④ ands on her!"

"There goe ⑤ e strange cow."

" _____ ! _____ _____ _____ _____ !"
① ② ③ ④ ⑤

SPELL WEAVING #2

Form a continuous thread of words in the grid by filling in the missing word from each caption, starting in the correspondingly numbered box and proceeding in the direction of the arrow in that box. Whenever you reach an edge, make a right-angle turn, following the direction shown by the arrow at the corner. Each word ends in the box before the next word's number. **ANSWER ON PAGE 141**

"I thought you said I should take the ball and slowly _____ around with it."

"We will begin with Schubert's 'Unfinished' Symphony, and that will be followed by Beethoven's 'Unwanted Sexual' _____ ."

"First of all, forget everything you learned in _____ school."

"I sometimes wish you'd stop referring to my career as 'a hitch in the _____ .'"

"Jalapeño was our first _____ to go platinum."

"Say, boss, could y' spare twen'y cents fer a _____?"

"An interesting selection, Dad, yet essentially a failure—as you can see, I'm still _____."

"You'd make a formidable _____."

"Big date tonight, Dad. Can I borrow the _____?"

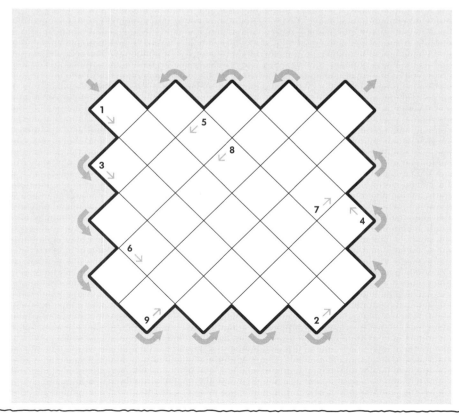

67 NAME THAT TUNE

Match each cartoon (1–13) to the song lyric (A–M) that serves as its caption. **ANSWER ON PAGE 141**

WORLD'S MOST BORING FOLK SINGER

A *"He knows when you are sleeping. He knows when you're awake."*

B *"Hey! Forget your troubles. Come on, get happy!"*

C *"Hey, good-lookin', whatcha got cookin'?"*

D *"I love a parade!"*

E *"I'm dreaming of a white Christmas."*

F *"It's beginning to look a lot like Christmas."*

G *"Just Molly and me, and baby makes three ..."*

H *"Ninety-nine bottles of beer on the wall, ninety-nine bottles of beer."*

I *"Oh, say, can you see by the dawn's early light ..."*

J *"Oops! There goes another rubber-tree plant!"*

K *"Take me out to the ballgame! I don't care if I never get back!"*

L *"You do the hokeypokey and you turn yourself around—that's what it's all about."*

M *"You've got to give a little, take a little, and let your poor heart break a little."*

Each letter in each of these captions has been replaced with the same digit every time it appears. You will need only the letters that are given below the coded caption for each cartoon. Use the patterns and word lengths to break each numerical code and reconstruct the caption. Each cartoon uses a different code.

ANSWER ON PAGE 141

1

"12345 34 678 5921958."

ABEGHINRT

2

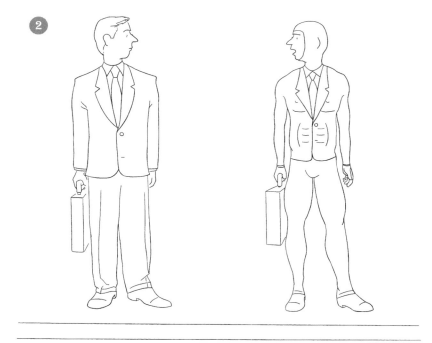

"12 3425 617 7851526938."

ACEINRSTU

3

"122341563 7356189 187143."

ADEGIMNST

4

"12345 356311272582."

CDEFGINR

This puzzle has two parts. Start by figuring out the word missing from each of the first six cartoons. Then determine what those words have in common with one another. That common element, in plural form, is what's been removed from the captionless cartoon in the box. (The original cartoon is shown with the puzzle's answer.) **ANSWER ON PAGE 141**

1

"It's dull now, but at the end they smash their instruments and set _____ to the chairs."

2

"And that's why we wear _____ suspenders."

3

"He's a real _____ of fortune. He's flown for Spain, China, and Pepsi-Cola."

4

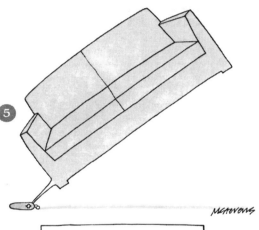

"Speaking as one blue-collar _____ , I'll tell you what I'm sick of. I'm sick of all these politicians pandering to my baser fears and prejudices."

5

SWISS _____ COUCH

6

"One last question, pending the new regulations. If I were a _____ and you were a lady, would you marry me anyway, would you have my baby?"

First determine the word missing from each of these nine captions. The nine words go into the grid in order, one letter per space, starting in the upper left square and spiraling inward. Each answer word overlaps the following answer word by at least one letter, so use neighboring answers to help solve the puzzle. (Every letter is used in two words, except at the beginning of the first word and the end of the last.) When all the answers have been filled in, the shaded column, reading down, will reveal the caption to the cartoon in the box above the grid. **ANSWER ON PAGE 141**

"If I'd known shopping could be this easy, I would have dressed up as a cop _____ ago!"

"Understand now? The ball must roll to the edge of the cup, _____ , and drop in."

"Now, stop me if I get to jabbering and _____ a war."

"The _____ American drinker consumes twenty-four gallons of beer per year, Foley, but not all in one night!"

"I happen to be a MacNab, Miss. I couldn't help noticing that you're wearing our _____ ."

"*Good evening. I'm Walt Fendow, who, after much infighting, kicking and scratching, politicking, backbiting, and throat-cutting, has finally emerged as your _____ .*"

"*I'll assume, then, my remarks have hit a responsive _____ ?*"

"*Might I rest now, Mr. _____ ?*"

"*I had a terrific _____ , but there's just no satisfying some people.*"

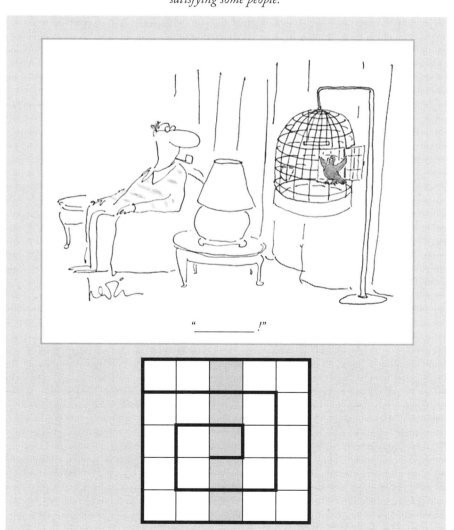

"*_____ !*"

To discover the caption to this Charles Addams cartoon, look at the eleven isolated pieces at right and find them in the large picture. (Some pieces have been rotated.) When you find a piece, write the letter coordinates showing where it came from—putting the column letter in the circle and the row letter in the square. When you've found them all, those letters, in order, will spell out the cartoon's caption.   **ANSWER ON PAGE 141**

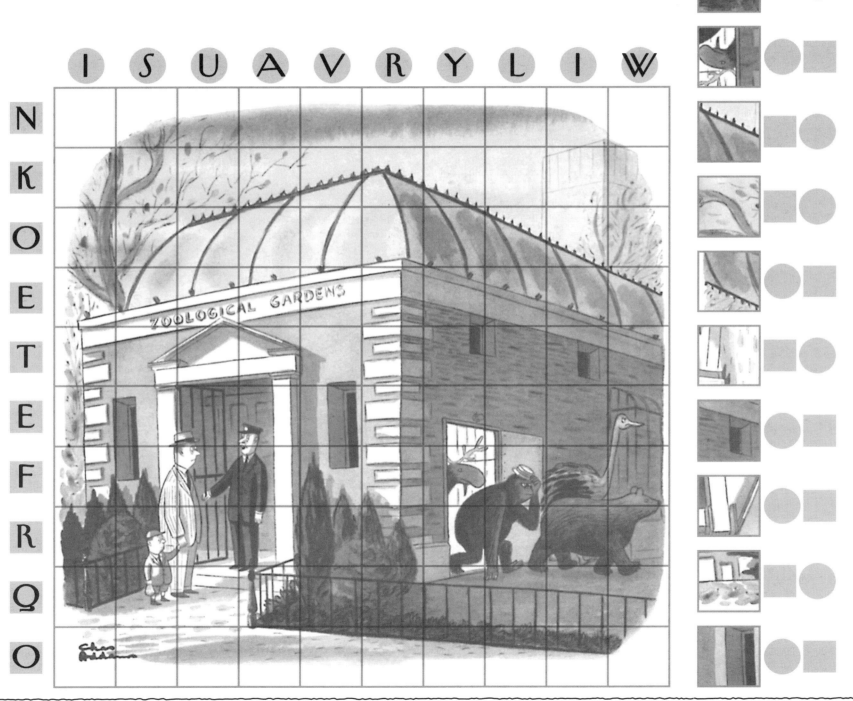

One word is missing from the caption to each of the first five cartoons here. Fill in the missing words, one letter per blank, and transfer the letters to the correspondingly numbered spaces in the box to fill in the caption for the final cartoon. Work back and forth to complete the puzzle.

ANSWER ON PAGE 141

"Now, here's something for a reader of

‾27‾ ‾35‾ ‾18‾ ‾8‾ ‾4‾ ‾20‾ ‾30‾ stories."

"I say it's genetically ‾2‾ ‾7‾ ‾16‾ ‾22‾ ‾33‾ ‾12‾ ‾31‾ ,
and I say the hell with it."

"In a further effort to ingratiate ‾9‾ ‾28‾ ‾25‾ ‾11‾ ‾21‾ ‾14‾ ‾5‾ with
New Yorkers, Hillary Clinton threw out the first pitch at last night's
Yankee game and went on to pitch three scoreless innings."

" ‾13‾ ‾15‾ ‾3‾ ‾24‾ ‾32‾ ‾19‾ ‾29‾ amnesia, Doc. Doesn't
know his name, but remembers the Alamo."

"Ask the judge whether we can find the defendant not guilty
and still ‾26‾ ‾23‾ ‾17‾ ‾1‾ ‾6‾ ‾34‾ ‾10‾ him."

"
‾1‾ ‾2‾ ‾3‾ ‾4‾ ‾5‾ ‾6‾ ‾7‾ , ‾8‾ ‾9‾ ‾10‾ ‾11‾ ‾12‾

‾13‾ ‾14‾ ‾15‾ ‾16‾ ‾17‾ ‾18‾ ‾19‾ ‾20‾ ‾21‾

‾22‾ ‾23‾ ‾24‾ ‾25‾ ‾26‾ ‾27‾ ‾28‾ ‾29‾ ‾30‾ ‾31‾ ‾32‾ ‾33‾ ‾34‾ ‾35‾ "

Two five-letter words that are related in some way are missing from the captions of cartoons 1 and 11. Start by entering these two words in the correspondingly numbered spaces in the grid. Then determine the five-letter words missing from the nine other captions here. They can be placed into the intermediate steps so that the word at the top changes into the word at the bottom, with a single letter changing at each step. If you get stuck, try solving from the bottom up.   **ANSWER ON PAGE 142**

"Sorry, but you're going to have to remind me who gets the red wine and who gets the _____?"

"My wife has grown fond of remarking, 'At retirement, they should name a _____ hole after you.'"

"Oops—I _____ I hit 'enter.'"

"With civilization on the _____ of annihilation, it's comforting to have it discussed, isn't it?"

"I've had to _____ hard for everything I've ever really wanted."

"Come here a minute, dear. Skeeter's learned a new _____ ."

"I wuz born in 1905. Then suddenly everything went _____ ."

"My father's gentler than _____ !"

"Love the exposed _____ ."

"I wish I had walls as _____ as this in my apartment."

"Either they've succeeded in completely cleaning up the industry or the set is on the _____ ."

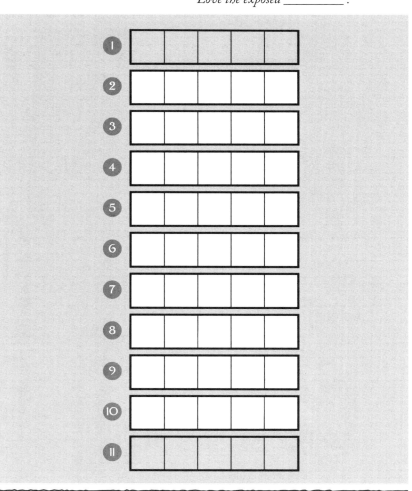

A cartoonist's style often changes over the years, either by evolution or intelligent design. Here are some of the more extreme examples of changing styles. On this page are cartoons taken from within the first year of nine cartoonists' appearances in *The New Yorker* (their names are listed in the box on the opposite page). Their signatures have been removed, but otherwise the cartoons are untouched. On the opposite page are examples of their work from decades later. Match the befores (1–9) with the afters (A–I).

ANSWER ON PAGE 142

"Darling, would it upset you terribly if I came out for peace?"
(1962)

"But it *is* half man and half horse."
(1941)

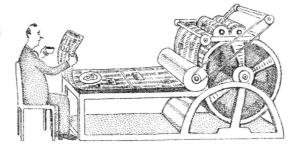

(1977)

"But surely you don't mean to imply that *this* wash is whiter!"
(1961)

"No, you're not disturbing me, Herb. I'm up with the chickens this morning."
(1977)

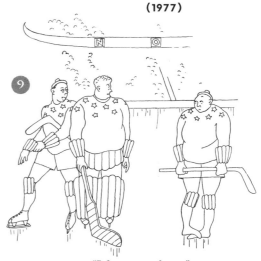

"He's been up a week now, and there's nothin' we can do about it."
(1932)

"Ketchup please."
(1925)

"My youngest is a terror. We can't do a thing with 'im."
(1930)

"I forgot my skates."
(1933)

"Hmm . . . any dietary restrictions?"
(2005)

"I do—but it might just be the liquor talking."
(2004)

"That's my Horace in 1957, just before he
lost his train of thought."
(1976)

"You wait here. I'll talk to him."
(1989)

Entomologist
(1987)

"No opinion? _You?_"
(1964)

"The security screener said I have
exquisite feet."
(2004)

"I'm not trying to sell you anything,
sir. I'm doing market research, and all
I ask is two or three hours of your time
to answer a few thousand questions."
(2000)

(1969)

THE CARTOONISTS

CHARLES ADDAMS	GEORGE PRICE
PETER ARNO	WILLIAM STEIG
LEO CULLUM	SAUL STEINBERG
J. B. HANDELSMAN	ROBERT WEBER
ROBERT MANKOFF	

Some captions are so funny that they evoke laughter independently of the cartoons that accompany them. These are not those captions. The captions here are, in fact, ordinary phrases. They become funny only when paired with their respective drawings. Match each picture (1–8) with its proper, if surprising, caption (A–H). **ANSWER ON PAGE 142**

①

②

③

④

⑤

⑥

⑦

⑧

A "As a matter of fact, you did catch us at a bad time."

B "Great coffee, honey!"

C "Honey, I'm home."

D "I have a couple of other projects I'm excited about."

E "O.K., I'm sitting. What is it?"

F "Paper or plastic?"

G "Stop me if you've heard this one before."

H "There's someone I'd like you to meet."

Drop the letters from each of the vertical columns into the empty boxes below them so that the cartoon's caption will read from left to right, line by line. For example, in caption 1 the letters P, I, W, and T (seen in the grid's first column) will appear in some order in the four blank boxes below them. Black squares indicate the ends of words. **ANSWER ON PAGE 142**

①

P	U	L			A	G							
I	H	M	T	D		O	A	E	W	A	N	R	N	T	R		D
W	O	A	N	Y		B	F	J	S	S	T	K	E	E	E	A	I	E	E
T	H	I	A	E	I	I	E	T	U	U	A	A	D	R	F	O	M	R	A

②

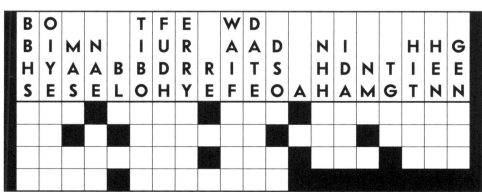

B	O				T	F	E		W	D								
B	I	M	N		T	I	U	R		A	A	D	N	I		H	H	G
H	Y	A	A	B	B	U	R	R	R	I	T	S			D	N	T	I	E	E
S	E	S	E	L	O	H	Y	E	F	E	O	A	H	A	M	G	T	N	N

In each caption, two words have each had a single letter changed to form two new words. The changed words can be found anywhere in the caption but do not involve incidental words or character names. Restore the captions by changing the letters back. **ANSWER ON PAGE 142**

3

"I wish I had a good defective stork."

1

"We're raisins the children as corks."

2

"Jack, when we get down the hill, let's put the sail up for suction."

4

"Mr. Hoover is out. Would you care to weave your fingerpaints?"

5

"Before I forget, Detrick, here's the denial play."

7

"Might I pound a note of caption?"

6

"You're in the wrong procession. They'd never name a candy bar after a fudge."

8

"The good news is that a delirious stick of perky is still a very affordable seventy-five cents."

E̲ach caption here is missing a different six-letter word. When correctly stacked in the grid, the six words will form a word square, with the same words reading down as across, in the same order. Work back and forth to complete the puzzle.

ANSWER ON PAGE 142

"She has her own _____ ."

"I can say this much. The new fall _____ is no giant step for mankind."

"Go ask your search _____ ."

"I've sown, I've _____ , and now what?"

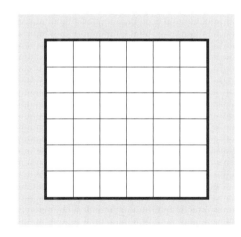

"I beg your pardon, Madam, but I happen to be an antique _____ , and I couldn't help noticing what excellent condition you're in."

"How long must I _____ this insult to my intelligence?"

Each caption here can be completed with a six-letter word, which is to be entered clockwise or counterclockwise around its corresponding number in the grid. The starting point of each word is indicated by a dot, but the direction of each answer is for you to determine.

ANSWER ON PAGE 142

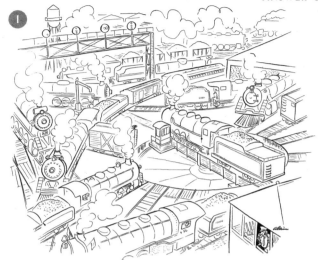

"Hello, Evening Journal? I'd like to speak to the Puzzle _____ ."

"I have to hang up now. You just _____ through the door."

"Forgive me, Doris, but some computer _____ from Roslyn, Long Island, has just gained access to my feelings."

"But, Magda, couldn't you _learn_ to _____ to me?"

"You're all _____ and no swash."

"We're replacing you with an _____ . So sorry."

"This is a little embarrassing to admit, but everything that happens happens for no real _____ ."

"I preferred their 'Take a _____ ' system."

"Old Man Connelly has been having considerable success with his _____ defense."

"It's deliciously _____ ."

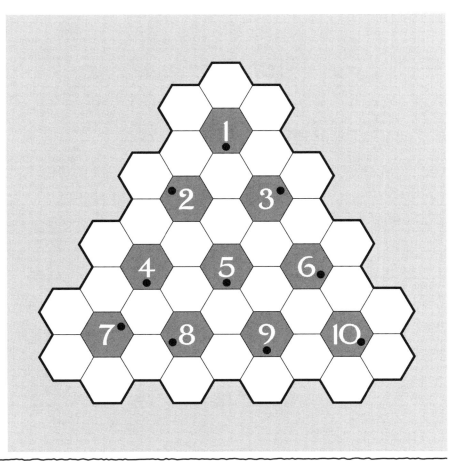

In the party game of charades, words are often formed by combining small phonetic chunks. In each equation here, the word missing from the first caption plus the word missing from the second caption, when spoken together, will sound like the word missing from the final caption, as in PACE + TREES = PASTRIES. Note that the word's sound, not its spelling, is the key to solving the puzzle.

ANSWER ON PAGE 142

1

_____ IN ACCOUNTING

+

"It's sixteen hundred dollars for August, including gas, electricity, maintenance, beach sticker, and old Mrs. Pennington up in the _____."

=

"Watch yourself, Celeste. They've got the _____ pilot on."

2

"There are times when I wonder if maybe I didn't _____ her too hard."

+

"Take this, Luke. They say it's impossible to get a decent baguette _____ of the Pecos."

=

"Pomp, greed, _____ , intrigue—it's been a fun year, hasn't it?"

3

"_____ !"

+

"I said the lid snapped my _____ off!"

=

"Come to bed, Ridgely. If your _____ were going to return, it would have been back hours ago."

Match each street vendor (1–9) with the item for sale that was originally announced on the cart or its umbrella (A–I). **ANSWER ON PAGE 142**

(A) **APPLES**	(F) **KWIK LOANS**
(B) **BEEFCAKE**	(G) **LAWSUITS**
(C) **BLUBBER**	(H) **LEFTOVERS**
(D) **BRUSSELS SPROUTS**	(I) **PLUTONIUM**
(E) **FIRST AID**	

Each of the captions on this page (1–8) is missing a five-letter word. Each of those words, when the order of its letters is reversed, can be fit into one of the spaces on the opposite page (A–H) to complete a new word. For example, the word ANNOY when reversed would fit into MA___ISE to complete the word MAYONNAISE.

ANSWER ON PAGE 142

1

"On the other hand, he _ _ _ _ _ _
takes a sick day."

2

"The little sad faces next to some _ _ _ _ _ _ _ _
mean they don't taste very good."

3

"O.K. with you if I eat that _ _ _ _ _ _ _ _
of wedding cake that's been in the freezer for
thirty years?"

4

"Come on, come on! Stop playing detective
and _ _ _ _ _ _ _ like the rest."

5

"Finally, we realized where all that
_ _ _ _ _ _ was coming from."

6

NOT SO _ _ _ _ _ _ _ STATISTICS

7

"See, that's your problem right there—the
roof is mostly _ _ _ _ _ _ _."

8

"Bad news—that fire in your belly is
an _ _ _ _ _ _ _."

"Hey, don't I get a R_ _ _ _ _ _ T ?"

"What's to P_ _ _ _ _ _ T some total stranger
anywhere in the world from paying my bills?"

"They've got me doing CO_ _ _ _ _ _ CS
research."

"What's so big about Harold Pinter? Our life was full of
P_ _ _ _ _ NT pauses long before he came along."

"Being man's best friend does not, in my case,
P_ _ _ _ _ _ DE having a feeling for an
attractive member of my own species, baby."

"Well, Mom, I've decided to leave home and seek
my fortune. Thanks a lot for all those years of
yummy bran MU_ _ _ _ _ _ ."

"Oh, knock it off! It's only cream of
ASPA_ _ _ _ _ _ ."

"And another feature—in case RE_ _ _ _ _ _ ES
should drop in unexpectedly, this absolutely cannot be
turned into a bed."

Each cartoon here contains the words "the end" somewhere in its caption.
Match the cartoons (1–8) with their captions (A–H).

ANSWER ON PAGE 142

A "… and your car will throw a rod two days after the end of the warranty period."

B "As far as I'm concerned, gentlemen, this marks the end of the Schwarzwälder String Quartet."

C "But I thought once the I.R.S. applied a penalty, that was the end of it."

D "Eddie was a simple man and, in the end, an eminently practical one."

E "Hey, look! Sixth row, tenth from the end! The blue one! That's _ours_!"

F "Oh dear! We'll never hear the end of this."

G "Why can't they save all the commercials to the end, and then we could be honor-bound to look at them?"

H "You're through, Merriweather. Clear your desk and be out of the building by the end of the day."

ANSWERS

BEFORE   AFTER

ZIEGLER

1 MIND READING

1. E	4. D	7. J	10. K
2. H	5. C	8. A	11. I
3. L	6. B	9. G	12. F

2 DOWN PLAY #1

① W R O N G
② B E D R O O M
③ P L U M B E R
④ B A L D N E S S

⑤ V E R T I C A L
⑥ S H O T G U N
⑦ E M E R G E N C Y
⑧ E R O T I C A
⑨ T E L E P H O N E

The caption to the final cartoon is *"Well, there goes lunch."*

3 TAKE FIVE #1

B	E	A	M	S
E	L	B	O	W
A	B	O	V	E
M	O	V	I	E
S	W	E	E	T

"Too SWEET. Use less revenge."
"Watch where you're shoving that ELBOW, Mac!"
"Well, so far I'm managing to stay ABOVE the fray."
"I think I can get you off with a lighter sentence, but it might screw up your MOVIE deal."
"In our first year of marriage we exposed our BEAMS, too."

4 ISOLATION BOOTH

The caption is *"Write about dogs!"*

5 DESK SET

1. K	5. J	9. F	13. A
2. D	6. B	10. C	
3. L	7. E	11. H	
4. G	8. I	12. M	

6 STEP BY STEP #1

1. *"Off with my HEAD!"*
2. *"Mitchell—HERD of four."*
3. *"We just haven't been flapping them HARD enough."*
4. *"If it please the Court, I have a get-out-of-jail-free CARD."*
5. *"As you can see, we've transferred your husband from intensive to casual CARE."*
6. *"I warned you it was lighthearted holiday FARE!"*
7. *"FORE!"*
8. *"We the jury award the plaintiff all the gold in FORT Knox."*
9. *"Your mother wanted you to have this for good luck. It's her FOOT."*

7 CROSSWORD #1

H	A	S			S	E	C	T	S		A	N	E	W
E	L	L	A		M	A	O	R	I		T	Y	R	O
R	O	O	M	S	E	R	V	I	C	E	H	E	R	E
	U	P	S	C	A	L	E			L	E	T	S	
		C	A	R	Y			P	A	I	N			
S	N	A	R	L	S		B	E	G		S	I	R	S
P	E	T	A	L		B	A	E	R	S		G	U	M
E	A	T	Y	O	U	R	B	R	O	C	C	O	L	I
A	L	E		P	R	I	E	S		H	O	T	E	L
K	E	N	T		S	A	L		R	E	M	A	D	E
	O	N	A	N		R	O	M	P					
N	A	U	T		D	O	G	E	A	R	S			
F	E	T	C	H	I	T	Y	O	U	R	S	E	L	F
U	H	O	H		S	E	N	S	E		S	P	A	R
R	I	P	E		M	E	E	T	S			S	T	Y

8 ONCE REMOVED #1

1. H	4. D	7. G	10. A
2. F	5. E	8. C	11. J
3. I	6. B	9. K	

9 BAR CODE

1. *"Why is it that the people in charge always turn out to be idiots? Present company, of course, excepted."*
2. *"Be reasonable, man. I'll be glad to explain the meaning of life, but not during rush hour."*
3. *"Double Scotches for me and my superego, and a glass of water for my id, which is driving."*
4. *"This place isn't bad during the week, but on weekends it turns into a zoo."*

10 PARTNERS IN RHYME #1

1. *"No, I would not care to go out and raid the CARROT PATCH with you."*
2. *"Now, now, Ruffy, if you'll spare me the threats I'll spare you the LEGAL JARGON."*
3. *"In case they should accept my book, I thought this photo would do nicely for the DUST JACKET."*
4. *"Just a heads up, Jack—I've invited the Navy to use my back yard for BOMBING PRACTICE."*
5. *"Sure, it's an eyesore, but we get BETTER TIME than anyone else in the neighborhood."*
6. *"This is a WATER PISTOL—I mean this is a stickup."*
7. *"All righty, then, let's move on to the NECK MUSCLES."*
8. *"I found the OLD FORMAT much more exciting."*

11 ACROSTIC #1

"A drawing is always dragged down to the level of its caption."
    —James Thurber

Captions:

"And then, to make a long story short, I thoughtlessly put a return ADDRESS on the ransom note."
"Ah! It's the WOODWIND family!"
"Once again, I'm asking you. How are we going to make our GETAWAY?"
"Don't panic. I'm just a sore THROAT."
JUVENILE Court
"Oh, how very FRENCH."
"I hear the streets are paved with GARBAGE."
"I can't explain it. I see that guy coming up the walkway and I go POSTAL."
"Hey, what if marriages had term LIMITS?"

12 MIDDLE MANAGEMENT

1. E (aisle, paisley)
2. A (oldie, soldier)
3. C (event, seventh)
4. B (ducat, educate)
5. G (latte, flatten)
6. F (clips, eclipse)
7. D (angst, gangsta)

13 WELL-ORDERED

B, G, E, H, D, A, F, C

14 BUILDING UP #1

1. Tire
2. Irate
3. Retain
4. Ingrate
5. Altering
6. Triangles
7. Earthlings

15 YOU CAN SAY THAT AGAIN

1. B and L
2. G and I
3. F and K
4. D and E
5. A and N
6. H and M
7. C and J

16 CHARADES #1

1. Purse + weighed = persuade
2. Sue + veneer = souvenir
3. Crow + shade = crocheted

17 TROPHY CASE

1. E
2. B
3. C
4. D
5. F
6. A

18 PYRAMID SCHEME #1

1. Perish
2. Thirst
3. Setter
4. Attack
5. Seurat
6. Tissue
7. Ticket
8. Icarus
9. Taurus
10. Saints

19 WRITTEN IN STONE

1. L
2. B
3. K
4. G
5. H
6. D
7. E
8. I
9. A
10. F
11. J
12. M
13. C
14. O
15. N

20 DROP ME A LINE #1

1. *"It's very gratifying, but there's a lot of responsibility that goes along with it."*
2. *"Sure, I'd get married again, but who wants a she-wolf with two adopted children?"*

21 TV TIME

1. 1980s
2. 1940s
3. 2000s
4. 1970s
5. 1960s
6. 1950s
7. 1990s
8. 1930s

22 SPELL WEAVING #1

1. Labyrinth
2. Inflatable
3. Evening
4. Likable
5. Leaving
6. Family
7. Elm
8. Beer
9. Flag

23 TAKE FIVE #2

C	R	O	S	S
R	I	C	H	E
O	C	E	A	N
S	H	A	R	D
S	E	N	D	S

"If you listen carefully, you can hear the OCEAN."
"Yes, but take away the rodent droppings and the occasional SHARD of glass, and you've still got a damn fine product."
"We CROSS the road tonight."
"The couple at Table Three SENDS you compliments. However, Tables Six and Fourteen are of a different mind entirely."
"Come on, honey. We may no longer be 'nouveau,' but at least we're still 'RICHE.'"

24 I NEED A CAPTION, STAT!

1. C
2. H
3. E
4. B
5. A
6. D
7. G
8. F

25 DOWN PLAY #2

The caption to the final cartoon is *"You'd love this part."*

26 FIT TO A TEE

1. F	3. A	5. C	7. E
2. B	4. H	6. G	8. D

27 TAKE A LETTER

1. *"Sorry, but all my power's been turned BACK to the STATES."*
2. *"Isn't it wonderful that the PRICE of CHIPS hasn't gone up at all?"*
3. *"They say there's nothing FINER for stimulating the ROOTS."*
4. *"A funny thing happened on my WAY into the GARAGE."*
5. *"He has my NOSE and his father's ANGER."*
6. *"I understand they MET at a PEASANT uprising."*
7. *"If I were a CAR, you could find the WORDS."*
8. *"Ah, not too bad. Nothing here that MONEY can't CURE."*

28 CROSSWORD #2

D	O	L	T		M	A	T	H		S	O	L
E	R	A	S		C	A	L	A	I	S		T	W	O

(Crossword grid reads:)

```
D O L T  M A T H  S O L
E R A S  C A L A I S  T W O
W E H A D A N A R G U M E N T
     R O P E S  H E A P S
S U B  S E T  A T T Y
A R A M I S  A L E  A I D A
F A D E D  G R I S T  T E N
A N D N O W H E S T R Y I N G
R I O  S H A N T  O S S I E
I A G O  O N A  B U L W E R
     U R S A  N A B  E S S
  S A T A N  B I B L E
T O M A K E M E F E E L B A D
A H A  E X A L T S  A U T O
N O N  T R A Y  N Y E T
```

29 GOOD HEAVENS!

1. I	4. K	7. C	10. B
2. F	5. H	8. E	11. J
3. G	6. L	9. A	12. D

30 AC-ROZ-TIC

"How does she know that these are cartoons?"

1. Shoes	6. Too
2. What's	7. Treat
3. He	8. Cheese
4. Woodstock	9. No
5. Answers	

31 A BUNCH OF BOZOS

1. C	3. H	5. F	7. E
2. B	4. A	6. D	8. G

32 BY THE NUMBERS #1

1. *"All I see is more trees."*
2. *"Small Caesar salad?"*
3. *"Eat lots of carrots."*
4. *"It needs additives."*

33 PYRAMID SCHEME #2

1. Heaven	6. Static
2. Cereal	7. Toupee
3. Reheat	8. Bottom
4. Bounce	9. Atomic
5. Timber	10. Scales

34 LOST AND FOUND

1. G (angel, chess)	5. B (thou, guesses)
2. A (time, centers)	6. C (chill, china)
3. E (tin, absent)	7. D (member, cat)
4. F (rubber, shy)	

35 LAYOVERS #1

1. Potty	4. Totem	7. Sewing
2. Types	5. Tempo	8. Winged
3. Pesto	6. Pose	9. Edge

The caption to the final cartoon is *"Tweet?"*

36 TAKE FIVE #3

"THINK!"

"Our stock just went up ten points on the rumor that I was replacing you all with burlap SACKS stuffed with straw."

"I just said that for COMIC effect."

"I think my indictment was just and when all the FACTS are known I will be proven guilty."

"ALOHA!"

37 MIXED BREED

I, C, D, H, A, F, G, B, E

38 SIGNING OFF

1. I	4. D	7. J	10. H
2. G	5. B	8. A	
3. F	6. E	9. C	

39 STEP BY STEP #2

1. *"Another decade or so, and it'll be WARM enough for us."*
2. *"I'm sorry, but you have to be here the minute the doors open if you want WORM."*
3. *"I really can't emphasize this enough, Peters—you no longer WORK here."*
4. *"Your constant cries to cut the PORK sadden me, Senator."*
5. *"Now who do I see about the sweetheart in every PORT?"*
6. *"Why don't you young people play POST Office?"*
7. *"Would it be possible for you to totally exaggerate how much it will COST and how long it will take, so we'll be pleasantly surprised at the end?"*
8. *"One final question: Do you now own or have you ever owned a fur COAT?"*
9. *"Good news—those lumps were just COAL."*
10. *"It's never been about money. It's about the COOL stuff money can buy."*

40 MINICROSTIC #1

"Personally, I prefer a PIANO bar."
"Oh, I've stepped on a few TOES in my lifetime."
"Just clean out the GUTTERS, Tony, and point the chimney."
"You've changed, Irma. You used to love SOUSA marches."
"Five thousand hours, and his vital SIGNS are still strong."

Final caption: *"It's a gorgeous sunset. Pass it on."*

41 EXECUTIVE SUITE

1. G	3. C	5. F	7. A
2. H	4. B	6. E	8. D

42 MIXED DOUBLES

1. Einstein, nineties
2. Please, asleep
3. Caterer, terrace
4. Bordello, doorbell
5. Piecrust, pictures
6. Nameless, salesmen

43 CROSSWORD #3: BARSOTTI EXAM

44 REMEMBER THE MAINFRAME

1. F	3. H	5. E	7. D
2. G	4. A	6. C	8. B

45 CODE OF HONOR

1. *"Forgive me if I don't shake hands. Everything I touch lately turns to gold."*
2. *"To me, the whole thing has been an object lesson in the difference between humor and satire."*
3. *"I told the cook I would prefer that she use some kind of artificial blackbird substitute."*
4. *"Well, if you won't abdicate, the least you can do is raise my allowance."*

46 DOWN PLAY #3

The caption to the final cartoon is *"Hon, where's the butter?"*

47 ACROSTIC #2

"I adore Rembrandt's drawings. I'm nuts about Van Gogh. My favorite artist now is Picasso."—William Steig

Captions:

"I'll give it to you straight, Babcock. You lack the killer INSTINCT."
"When my time comes, I hope I can go with that same air of jaunty BRAVADO."
"That's pork—the meat of the pig. It makes an excellent substitute for TOFU."
"Keep it under your hat, but when this crowd thins out, I have some MARSHMALLOWS."
"Más AGUA for the gringos?"
"Fill'er up with TESTOSTERONE."
"Sorry, Akhet, but we've decided to stick with PYRAMIDS."
Henry VIII discloses his dream life to a psychoanalyst.
"I'm right on the fringe of a BIGGIE, R.B. I'm just waiting for it to jell."
"Gentlemen, it's time we gave some serious thought to the effects of global WARMING."
"It's the people DOWNSTAIRS again."

48 YOU CAN COUNT ON ME

1. G	4. C	7. E	10. J
2. I	5. F	8. A	
3. H	6. B	9. D	

49 BUILDING UP #2

1. Ten
2. Rent
3. Toner
4. Orient
5. Pointer
6. Proteins
7. Inspector
8. Receptions

50 DROP ME A LINE #2

1. *"It certainly is amazing what our scientists can reconstruct from just a few bones and fragments."*
2. *"You're right as rain. It's the dawn of history, and there are no clichés as yet. I'll drink to that!"*

51 CHAIN OF THOUGHT

1. Outside
2. Sidekick
3. Kickback
4. Backhand
5. Handgun
6. Gunfire
7. Firelight
8. Lighthouse
9. Housework
10. Workout

52 JACK IN THE BOX

1. J	5. F	9. E	13. A
2. N	6. M	10. P	14. G
3. C	7. O	11. K	15. H
4. L	8. B	12. I	16. D

53 TAKE SIX #1

M	A	P	L	E	S
A	R	R	E	S	T
P	R	E	T	T	Y
L	E	T	H	A	L
E	S	T	A	T	E
S	T	Y	L	E	S

"And to whom do you wish to leave the bulk of your ESTATE, sir?"

"Sure I told you not to worry your PRETTY little head about money, but that was ten years ago."

"Eddie is under house ARREST."

"I don't want to seem nosy, folks, but those aren't sugar MAPLES."

"Why have we come? Because only Earth offers the rock-bottom prices and wide selection of men's, women's, and children's clothing in the STYLES and sizes we're looking for."

"LETHAL injection's my favorite, because they don't make you shave your head."

54 PRICE COMPARISON

The caption is *"All rise."*

The differences in the bottom picture, from left to right, are: hair curler is missing, slipper is longer, cat is looking up, shapes on lamp's pole are switched, dog's tail has moved, colors are switched in hat on woman in picture, standing boy's sleeve is long, man's collar is a V-neck, edge of armrest is missing.

55 IMAGINE THAT!

1. I	4. D	7. B
2. F	5. H	8. A
3. E	6. G	9. C

56 STEP BY STEP #3

1. *"He makes it look so damn EASY."*
2. *"Gosh, is this part of the all-expense Middle EAST tour?"*
3. *"Somehow they don't seem to be selling as FAST as they should."*
4. *"Burglars, con men, and swindlers all over the place, and I have to marry a lousy accessory after the FACT."*
5. *"Would you like to take your old FACE?"*
6. *"No, no, Agnes! This is mine. You paid the bus FARE."*
7. *"Perhaps Monsieur would CARE for something more expensive?"*
8. *"The minute I saw this CARP, Mrs. Mugler, I thought of you."*
9. *"That's the first time I've heard 'My Way' played on a HARP."*
10. *"But she'll come down eventually, and she'll come down HARD."*

57 CROSSWORD #4: SHOUT!

D	O	D	G	E		L	I	A	R		C	O	B	
I	N	O	I	L		A	N	Y	A		S	H	U	E
L	A	N	D	L	U	B	B	E	R		P	E	C	S
L	I	N	D		T	O	E		E	P	O	C	H	S
	R	E	Y	N	A	R	D		L	A	R	K		
		A	A	H		P	O	R	T	M	A	N		
C	O	O	P	S		C	I	A	O		S	A	G	A
A	P	B		T	A	L	L	Y	H	O		T	U	G
R	A	J	A		P	A	L	S		O	B	E	Y	S
B	L	E	S	S	E	D			C	P	U			
	C	S	I				A	P	O	S	T	L	E	
A	T	T	I	R	E		N	O	R		C	E	L	S
H	A	I	G		G	E	S	U	N	D	H	E	I	T
A	X	O	N		G	L	E	N		S	E	R	T	A
B	I	N			S	O	L	D		C	R	Y	E	R

58 MINICROSTIC #2

"How about conjuring up something to take the drudgery out of WASHDAY?"

ACCOUNTANTS just want to have fun....

"I can see you drew HEAVILY from your own bad writing."

"It's a little present I gave myself for being so RICH."

"I give him two more minutes. Then I say so much for TELEKINESIS!"

Final caption: *"I always have chicken so I can study the entrails."*

59 CALL TO ORDER

1. 1970s	3. 1940s	5. 1960s	7. 2000s
2. 1990s	4. 1980s	6. 1950s	8. 1930s

60 ONCE REMOVED #2

1. J	4. F	7. B	10. E
2. H	5. D	8. A	11. I
3. C	6. K	9. G	

61 BY THE NUMBERS #2

1. *"Not apple pie again!"*
2. *"Let the healing begin!"*
3. *"Easter was last week."*
4. *"Innocence is no excuse."*

62 PARTNERS IN RHYME #2

1. *"HICKORY SMOKE—that's what gives it that hearty Western flavor."*
2. *"I'm writing my autobiography, to set the RECORD STRAIGHT."*
3. *"THIRTY DAYS. And, by the way, that was a very nice rendition of 'Feelings.'"*
4. *"Gee, Tommy, I'd be lost without your constant PEER PRESSURE."*
5. *"Oh, definitely, I feel there's a reason I was given a SECOND CHANCE."*
6. *"Melanie, this is my husband, Greg, and Greg's jacket from a PREVIOUS MARRIAGE."*
7. *"Every year a HUMBLE SHEPHERD! Can't he ever be one of the kings?"*
8. *"No, we aren't experiencing low VOTER TURNOUT. Everybody's here."*

63 THAT'S JUST GROSS!

1. K	5. A	9. G	13. D
2. J	6. M	10. C	14. F
3. N	7. I	11. B	
4. L	8. E	12. H	

64 LAW AND DISORDER

E, G, C, A, H, F, B, D, I

65 BUNCHLINES

1. *"I sleep half tHE Year—how much more space do you need?"*
2. *"Straighten thaT HAT, Soldier! Button that collar! I have spoken."*
3. *"How can yOU Read that garbage?"*
4. *"Wow! Dig the umbrelLA STands on her!"*
5. *"There goeS ONe strange cow."*

Final caption: *"Hey! That's our last son!"*

66 SPELL WEAVING #2

1. Meander	6. Malted
2. Obedience	7. Awake
3. Overture	8. Enemy
4. Bagel	9. Cardigan
5. Navy	

67 NAME THAT TUNE

1. D	5. A	9. B	13. L
2. E	6. F	10. M	
3. G	7. I	11. H	
4. K	8. J	12. C	

68 BY THE NUMBERS #3

1. *"Bring in the garbage."*
2. *"It cuts air resistance."*
3. *"Immediate seating inside."*
4. *"Feign indifference!"*

69 THE COMMON TOUCH

1. Fire	3. Soldier	5. Army
2. Red	4. Worker	6. Carpenter

These are all types of ants, which are shown below in the original cartoon.

70 LAYOVERS #2

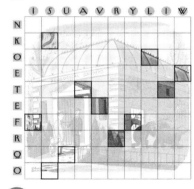

1. Waver	4. Start	7. Chord
2. Average	5. Tartan	8. Dali
3. Ages	6. Anchor	9. Alibi

The caption to the final cartoon is *"Voilà!"*

71 SPLITTING ADDAMS

The caption is *"Sorry, folks, we quit at five."*

72 MINICROSTIC #3

"Now, here's something for a reader of MYSTERY stories."

"I say it's genetically ALTERED, and I say the hell with it."

"In a further effort to ingratiate HERSELF with New Yorkers, Hillary Clinton threw out the first pitch at last night's Yankee game and went on to pitch three scoreless innings."

"PARTIAL amnesia, Doc. Doesn't know his name, but remembers the Alamo."

"Ask the judge whether we can find the defendant not guilty and still EXECUTE him."

Final caption: *"Careful, these plates are extremely dirty."*

73 STEP BY STEP #4

1. *"My wife has grown fond of remarking, 'At retirement, they should name a BLACK hole after you.'"*
2. *"I wuz born in 1905. Then suddenly everything went BLANK."*
3. *"Either they've succeeded in completely cleaning up the industry or the set is on the BLINK."*
4. *"With civilization on the BRINK of annihilation, it's comforting to have it discussed, isn't it?"*
5. *"Love the exposed BRICK."*
6. *"Come here a minute, dear. Skeeter's learned a new TRICK."*
7. *"I wish I had walls as THICK as this in my apartment."*
8. *"Oops—I THINK I hit 'enter.'"*
9. *"My father's gentler than THINE!"*
10. *"I've had to WHINE hard for everything I've ever really wanted."*
11. *"Sorry, but you're going to have to remind me who gets the red wine and who gets the WHITE?"*

74 CHANGING HANDS

1. I (Saul Steinberg)
2. A (Robert Mankoff)
3. G (Robert Weber)
4. C (George Price)
5. H (J. B. Handelsman)
6. B (Leo Cullum)
7. F (Peter Arno)
8. E (William Steig)
9. D (Charles Addams)

75 SURPRISE!

1. H
2. B
3. C
4. G
5. E
6. A
7. D
8. F

76 DROP ME A LINE #3

1. *"I may be awake for a while. I just dreamed that I ate an entire pound of sugar."*
2. *"His life was hanging by a thread, and then somebody fed him the bean burrito."*

77 SMALL CHANGE

1. *"We're RAISING the children as FORKS."*
2. *"Jack, when we get down the hill, let's put the PAIL up for AUCTION."*
3. *"I wish I had a good DETECTIVE STORY."*
4. *"Mr. Hoover is out. Would you care to LEAVE your FINGERPRINTS?"*
5. *"Before I forget, Detrick, here's the DENTAL PLAN."*
6. *"You're in the wrong PROFESSION. They'd never name a candy bar after a JUDGE."*
7. *"Might I SOUND a note of CAUTION?"*
8. *"The good news is that a DELICIOUS stick of JERKY is still a very affordable seventy-five cents."*

78 TAKE SIX #2

"She has her own AGENDA."
"I can say this much. The new fall LINEUP is no giant step for mankind."
"Go ask your search ENGINE."
"I beg your pardon, Madam, but I happen to be an antique DEALER, and I couldn't help noticing what excellent condition you're in."
"How long must I ENDURE this insult to my intelligence?"
"I've sown, I've REAPED, and now what?"

79 PYRAMID SCHEME #3

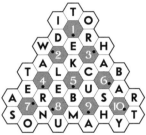

1. Editor
2. Walked
3. Hacker
4. Relate
5. Buckle
6. Abacus
7. Reason
8. Number
9. Ambush
10. Trashy

80 CHARADES #2

1. Autumn + attic = automatic
2. Conk + west = conquest
3. Boo + meringue = boomerang

81 THE WORD ON THE STREET

1. B
2. E
3. H
4. G
5. F
6. I
7. A
8. C
9. D

82 REVERSE ENGINEERING

1. B (never, prevent)
2. C (items, cosmetics)
3. A (piece, receipt)
4. F (sniff, muffins)
5. D (anger, pregnant)
6. H (vital, relatives)
7. G (sugar, asparagus)
8. E (ulcer, preclude)

83 THE END

1. G
2. B
3. H
4. A
5. F
6. D
7. C
8. E

INDEX OF ARTISTS

PUZZABILITY is a puzzle-writing company consisting of Robert Leighton (a *New Yorker* cartoonist), Mike Shenk, and Amy Goldstein, who somehow have worked a combined 60 years in the puzzle business. Puzzability creates puzzles for Web sites, major newspapers and magazines, ads and packaging, game shows, and other media.

WILL SHORTZ (Foreword) is the crossword editor of the *New York Times* and the puzzlemaster for NPR's "Weekend Edition Sunday." He is the author or editor of more than 150 books, including "The Puzzlemaster Presents" (vols. 1 and 2), "Will Shortz's Tournament Crosswords," and "Will Shortz's Best Brain Busters."

ROBERT MANKOFF (Foreword) is the cartoon editor of *The New Yorker* and the founder and president of the Cartoon Bank. He is a cartoonist, the author of a book on cartooning and creativity called "The Naked Cartoonist," and the editor of "The Complete Cartoons of the New Yorker" and other collections.